D0622045

Teaching with Books That Heal

Authentic Literature and Literacy Strategies to Help Children Cope with Everyday Problems

Patricia Liotta Kolencik, Ed.D.
Carianne Bernadowski, Ph.D.

Linworth Books

**Professional Development Resources for
K-12 Library Media and Technology Specialists**

Library of Congress Cataloging-in-Publication Data

Kolencik, Patricia Liotta.
  Teaching with books that heal : authentic literature and literacy strategies to help children cope
with everyday problems / Patricia Liotta Kolencik, Carianne Bernadowski.
      p. cm.
  Includes bibliographical references and index.
  ISBN 1-58683-220-4 (pbk.)
  1. Moral education (Elementary) 2. Character--Study and teaching (Elementary)--Activity pro-
grams--United States. 3. Children--Books and reading--United States. I. Bernadowski, Carianne.
II. Title.
  LC311.K65 2007
  370.11'4--dc22
                                            2006033591

Published by Linworth Publishing, Inc.
3650 Olentangy River Road
Columbus, Ohio 43214

Copyright © 2007 by Linworth Publishing, Inc.

All rights reserved. Purchasing this book entitles a librarian to reproduce activity sheets for use in
the library within a school or entitles a classroom teacher to reproduce activity sheets for single
classroom use within a school. Standard citation information should appear on each page. The
reproduction of any part of this book for an entire school or school system or for commercial use is
strictly prohibited. No part of this book may be electronically reproduced, transmitted or recorded
without written permission from the publisher.

ISBN: 1-58683-220-4

5 4 3 2 1

Table of Contents

Table of Contents continued

Table of Contents continued

Table of Contents continued

Table of Contents continued

Table of Figures

Table of Figures continued

About the Authors

 **Patricia Liotta Kolencik** is an assistant professor in the Teacher Education Department at Clarion University of Pennsylvania, Clarion, Pennsylvania. Prior to teaching at Clarion University, she was a high school librarian for 27 years. She holds a Doctorate in Education from the University of Pittsburgh, Pittsburgh, Pennsylvania, a M.A. from the University of Alabama, Tuscaloosa, Alabama, and a B.S.Ed. from Edinboro University of Pennsylvania. Kolencik has authored numerous articles for various scholarly and professional journals, including *Library Media Connection* and has been a contributing author to Linworth's *Skills for Life,* 2nd Edition as well as a manuscript reviewer.

 **Carianne Bernadowski** is an instructor in the Education Department at Clarion University. She earned a Ph.D. in Reading at The University of Pittsburgh. Prior to teaching at Clarion University, she was a literacy coordinator, reading specialist, and middle school language arts teacher. She holds a M.A. in Reading Education from Slippery Rock University of Pennsylvania, Slippery Rock, Pennsylvania, and a B.A. in Journalism and Communications/ Secondary Education from Point Park College, Pittsburgh, Pennsylvania. Bernadowski has authored several articles for *Teaching K-8, PA Reads* and *Teaching Tolerance.* She also serves as an educational consultant in the area of reading education for school districts.

Acknowledgments

We wish to gratefully acknowledge our loving husbands, Anthony Kolencik and Brian Bernadowski, and son, Maxwell Bernadowski, as well as other family members for their tireless support, encouragement, patience, and tolerance.

Introduction

Bullying. Death. Peer acceptance. Accepting differences. Adoption. Divorce. These pervasive issues are only a few of the personal challenges that many children experience and must deal with on a daily basis. This book provides elementary librarians and teachers with a compendium of quality children's book selections with accompanying reproducible literacy lessons as well as annotated books lists whose developmental themes reflect a variety of situations, conflicts, and emotions that trouble and challenge children. The quality book selections featured in this book have the potential to address children's heartaches, to help "dry the tears," and, more importantly, to build character, self-reliance, and resilience through the use of research-based literacy lessons that accompany each book selection.

A Word About the Purpose of the Book

We know that children's emotional distress is not checked at the school door. We are sensitive to the fact that all educators are confronted on a daily basis with the clamoring human reality of children whose hearts are broken as a result of a personal quandary. We hope that librarians and teachers are not licensed psychologists or therapists, but rather are caring individuals with warm hearts. This book will assist them with the hidden curriculum that addresses social learning concepts to build students' muscle of resilience. This book is by no means intended to be a bibliotherapeutic substitute for professional counseling, but is a text to "lend a helping hand." We believe librarians will reach for this book when filling requests for stories to help children develop self-reliance.

This book was written in response to the repeated question we hear in our professional work from school library media specialists and teachers everywhere. "Is there a book with ready-to-use activities I can use in the library or classroom to give children insight into significant life events such as death, divorce, or peer acceptance?" We believe this book will fill the need for a publication that can assist school library media specialists, teachers, and other educators as well as parents in guiding and nurturing children's special issues and concerns such as bullying or death of a family member. Age-appropriate literature can support children with the increasing number of potentially upsetting experiences they may face and help them survive and thrive.

Elementary librarians will find this book indispensable for several reasons. First, the book provides a distinctive opportunity for collaboration with classroom teachers and other members of the learning community to develop and teach information literacy skills, literacy/language arts skills, and technology skills.

Second, the annotated book lists that appear at the end of each chapter highlight award-winning titles, multicultural titles, and diverse authors including African Americans, Hispanics, Asians, Native Americans, and other cultural groups within American society to promote global interconnectedness, cultural awareness, and cultural heritage that appeal to all learners including English language learners and learners with special needs. School library media specialists can use these lists as 1) a tool for acquisitions for both the regular collection and the professional library collection; 2) a source to create book displays; 3) a bibliography to circulate among classroom teachers, school counselors, and other members of the learning community; 4) a source for book talks; and 5) a tool for professional development.

Third, the book selections along with the literacy lessons provide a springboard for librarians and teachers to initiate not only conversations on a professional level, but also to initiate dialogue with children to explore and define their feelings and emotions as they journey through life.

A Word About the Intended Audience

The primary audience for this book targets elementary school library media specialists and classroom teachers who work with kindergarten through sixth grade and other members of the learning community such as guidance counselors and school psychologists who work with elementary students. Additionally, this book will be of value to parents and to those who home school.

Format

The front matter contains a Standards Alignment Chart. The Standards Alignment Chart lists the individual lesson, project, or task that accompanies the featured books within the chapter. Additionally, the AASL/AECT's Information Literacy Standards for Student Learning and the NCTE/IRA's Standards for English Language Arts in their entirety are provided for quick reference for librarians and classroom teachers.

Each chapter features three developmentally appropriate, realistic fiction book selections related to the chapter's topic. For each selection, a summary of the story is given as well as a list of pre-reading vocabulary words found within the story. Each book selection is accompanied by a number of standards-based literacy lessons that include technology components. Each researched-based literacy lesson is divided into four segments:

1. DISCOVERY AND DISCUSSION: SETTING THE STAGE FOR READING
2. EXPLORATION: DURING READING
3. READING BETWEEN THE LINES: POST READING
4. BEYOND THE TEXT: LESSON EXTENSIONS

These four segments pose metacognitive and reflective activities to promote empathy and understanding, and reflect best practices of effective teaching and technology integration. Chapter One features books on bullying. Chapter Two presents selections on peer acceptance. Chapter Three provides selections on accepting differences. Chapters Four, Five, and Six include books on the loss of a family member, loss of a friend, and loss of a pet respectively. Chapter Seven focuses on adoption. Chapter Eight introduces book selections on divorce.

A section entitled, Additional Book Selections, Professional Resources, and Web Connections is found at the end of each chapter. These sections are divided into three segments:

1. children's fiction books

2. informational resources that are suggested selections for the professional library collection

3. several quality Web sites dealing with the chapter's topic.

The annotations of the fiction books vary in length and include a story summary. The majority of the annotations are the CIP descriptions from the Library of Congress. Each annotation has been assigned a recommended age level. The age level range was determined by publishers' designations. Estimates were given in the absence of publisher's information. Additionally, any type of award recognition is indicated. We also noted titles that are multicultural selections. At the time of this publication, all books were in print and Web sites were available. School library media specialists will find this section invaluable for collection development purposes and as a quick, reproducible bibliography to distribute to teachers and counselors.

Book Selections

Many children's books are available in the subject areas of bullying, peer acceptance, unique differences, death, adoption, and divorce, highlighting some of the best is our primary intent. By using a number of standard library book selection tools such as *Library Media Connection, Booklist, Horn Book, H. W. Wilson's Children's Catalog, School Library Journal, Brodart's Elementary School Library Collection,* and *Bulletin for the Center for Children's Books*, we selected the children's books and authors used in this work from recent children's literature, timeless classics, and award-winning and honor titles such as Caldecott, Newbery, Coretta Scott King, American Library's Notable Children's Books, and School Library Journal's Best Books of the Year.

The framework for selection of relevant titles was based on the following criteria:

1. the book's capacity to empathize with children and allow for self-understanding, encourage self-reliance, define feelings and emotions to enhance communication and add relevance to children's lives

2. the book's recognition by authorities who define quality, award-winning children's literature books whose themes are developmentally appropriate in the cognitive and affective domains

3. books whose characters are credible and authentic and have universal appeal

4. books whose vocabulary is rich, increases language development, and contain other high quality literary elements

5. books whose visual elements are of high literary artistic quality.

Additionally, our educational backgrounds in basic education and our professional experiences augmented the criteria for the selection.

The intent of the realistic fiction books selected in this resource is bibliographical and not bibliotherapeutic in nature. We want to provide a discussion of themes that allow for an examination of children's special concerns in a nonthreatening way, and present inherent book selections to promote good feelings and good relationships for children to become strong and emotionally secure.

Literacy Lessons

This book reinforces the literacy-coaching concept through its standards-based, researched-based reading and writing lessons that accompany each book selection. The literacy strategies employed in the lessons combine problem-based, inquiry-based, and project-based design based on the information literacy process. Additionally, the strategies promote student-generated comprehension that enriches social learning for all learners including English language learners, learners with special needs, and other at-risk students.

The literacy lessons can be viewed through two lenses. The first is to promote individual lifelong learning skills as outlined in the American Association of School Librarians/Association for Educational Communications and Technology's Information Literacy Standards for Student Learning and the National Council for Teachers of English/International Reading Association's Standards for English Language Arts. The second is to promote constructivist pedagogical values of collaboration, personal autonomy and relevance, generativity, reflectivity, and active engagement (Lebow, 1992, p. 5).

Bibliography

A bibliography of resources consulted to prepare this book is provided for further reference. Title and author indices are also included.

Standards Alignment Chart

Book Selection	Activity	Information Literacy Standards for Student Learning	NCTE/IRA Standards for English Language Arts
Hooway for Wodney Wat	The Letter R Scavanger Hunt	3, 4, 6, 9	1, 4, 5, 11, 12
	Animal Identification	1, 2, 3, 4, 6, 8, 9	1, 3, 4, 5, 6, 7, 8, 11, 12
	Reinforcement of the Letter R	4, 5, 6, 9	1, 3, 11, 12
	Feelings Chart	1, 2, 5, 6, 9	1, 3, 4, 11, 12
	Animal Alliteration Book	1, 3, 4, 5, 9	4, 5, 6, 11, 12
	Revisiting the Text/ Comprehension Questions	1, 2, 3, 6, 9	1, 3, 4, 11, 12
	Anti-bullying Poster	1, 3, 4, 5, 6, 7, 9	1, 4, 5, 6, 7, 11, 12
	Bully Box	1, 2, 4, 5, 6, 7, 9	1, 3, 4, 7, 11, 12
The Sissy Duckling	Musical Chairs	3, 4, 5, 6, 9	4, 5, 11, 12
	Classroom Community	6, 9	1, 6, 11, 12
	Beach Ball Comprehension	1, 2, 6, 9	1, 3, 4, 11, 12
	Dissecting a Character	1, 2, 3, 4, 6, 7, 9	1, 3, 4, 11, 12
	Readers Theater	1, 2, 3, 4, 5, 6, 7, 9	1, 3, 4, 5, 6, 8, 11, 12
	Compare/Contrast Diagram	1, 2, 3, 6, 9	1, 3, 4, 11, 12
	What Is the Consequence?	1, 2, 3, 4, 6, 9	1, 3, 4, 11, 12
	Working with Onsets and Rimes	1, 7, 9	4, 6, 11, 12
	Making Words	1, 7, 9	4, 6, 11, 12
	Egg Hero Descriptive Writing	1, 3, 4, 5, 9	4, 5, 6, 11, 12
	Write a Book Review	1, 2, 3, 5, 8	4, 5, 6, 8, 11, 12
Goggles	Preparing to Read	2, 3, 7, 9	4, 11, 12
	Prereading Questions	2, 3, 7, 9	4, 11, 12
	Story Imaging	1, 3, 6	1, 3, 11, 12
	Flannel Board	1, 2, 3, 6	1, 2, 4, 11, 12
	Book Boxes	1, 2, 3, 4, 5, 9	1, 3, 4, 5, 6, 7, 11, 12
	Checking for Comprehension: Discussion Questions	4, 5, 7, 9	1, 3, 4, 11, 12
	Bumper Sticker	1, 3, 4, 6, 9	4, 5, 6, 11, 12
	Character Comparison/Contrast	1, 2, 5, 6	1, 3, 4, 11, 12
	Developing Dialogue	1, 2, 3, 4, 5, 6, 9	1, 3, 4, 5, 6, 11, 12
	Book Jacket Design	1, 2, 3, 4, 5, 6, 9	1, 3, 4, 5, 6, 11, 12
Elmer	Consonant Variations	1, 2, 6, 9	6, 11, 12
	I Am Unique	3, 5, 9	4, 6, 11, 12
	Flipbook Summary	1, 3, 4, 9	1, 3, 4, 5, 6, 11, 12
	Patchwork Quilt	1, 2, 3, 5, 9	1, 3, 4, 5, 6, 11, 12
	Writing a Sequel	1, 3, 4, 6, 8, 11, 12	1, 3, 4, 5, 6, 8, 11, 12
	Elephant Detectives	1, 2, 3, 4, 6, 7, 8, 9	1, 3, 4, 5, 6, 7, 8, 11, 12
Horace and Morris, but Mostly Dolores	Prereading/Predicting	1, 2, 6, 9	3, 4, 11, 12
	Syllabication	1, 2, 9	4, 11, 12
	Phoneme/Sound Manipulation	1, 2, 9	4, 11, 12
	Checking for Comprehension: Discussion Questions	4, 5, 7, 9	1, 3, 4, 11, 12
	Rhyming Game	1, 2, 3, 9	4, 11, 12
	Dialogue Writing	1, 2, 6, 9	3, 4, 5, 6, 11, 12
	Sequencing	1, 2, 3, 6, 9	1, 3, 4, 11, 12

Book Selection	Activity	Information Literacy Standards for Student Learning	NCTE/IRA Standards for English Language Arts
	Author Study	1, 2, 3, 4, 5, 6, 8, 9	1, 3, 4, 7, 8, 11, 12
	Letter Writing	1, 2, 3, 6, 9	4, 5, 6, 11, 12
The Brand New Kid	Friendship Outline	1, 2, 3, 4, 5, 9	4, 5, 6, 11, 12
	Rhyme Find	1, 2, 3, 4, 5, 6, 9	1, 3, 4, 6, 11, 12
	Shower Curtain Rhyme Toss	1, 2, 3, 4, 5, 6, 9	1, 3, 4, 6, 11, 12
	Bookmark Book Report	1, 3, 4, 5, 9	3, 4, 5, 6, 11, 12
	Writing Prompts	3, 5, 9	4, 5, 6, 11, 12
	Welcome Letter/PowerPoint™ Presentation	1, 2, 3, 4, 5, 6, 8, 9	4, 5, 6, 8, 11, 12
	Synonyms/Antonyms	1, 3, 4, 5, 9	4, 5, 6, 11, 12
	Word Wall Wizard	1, 3, 4, 5, 9	4, 5, 6, 11, 12
Looking After Louis	Prereading/Prediction	1, 2, 6, 9	3, 4, 11, 12
	Using a Venn Diagram	2, 3, 4, 5, 6, 9	3, 7, 11, 12
	Puppet Retelling	1, 2, 5, 6	1, 3, 4, 7, 11, 12
	Writing Prompts	3, 5, 9	4, 5, 6, 11, 12
	Checking for Comprehension: Discussion Questions	4, 5, 7, 9	1, 3, 4, 11, 12
	Point of View	1, 2, 3, 5, 6, 7, 9	1, 3, 4, 5, 6, 11, 12
	Creating Words from a Name	3, 5, 9	11, 12
	Recess Survey	1, 2, 3, 5, 6, 7, 9	1, 3, 4, 5, 6, 7, 11, 12
The Ugly Duckling	Prereading	3, 4, 9	4, 11, 12
	What Do We Already Know?	3, 4, 9	4, 11, 12
	Prediction of Vocabulary	3, 5, 9	11, 12
	Story Hand	4, 5, 7, 9	1, 3, 4, 11, 12
	Checking for Comprehension: Discussion Questions	4, 5, 7, 9	1, 3, 4, 11, 12
	Duckling Poem	1, 2, 3, 4, 5, 9	1, 3, 4, 5, 6, 11, 12
	Readers Theater/Create a Mask	1, 2, 3, 4, 5, 6, 7, 9	1, 3, 4, 5, 6, 8, 11, 12
Oliver Button Is a Sissy	Exploring Gender Stereotyping	1, 2, 6, 9	5, 11, 12
	Story Comprehension	4, 5, 7, 9	1, 3, 4, 11, 12
	Class Brick Wall	1, 2, 3, 4, 5, 6, 8, 9	1, 3, 4, 5, 6, 7, 8, 11, 12
	Story Sharing Retelling	1, 2, 5, 6, 7, 9	1, 3, 4, 7, 11, 12
	Sissy Acrostic Super Words	1, 3, 4, 5, 9	4, 5, 6, 11, 12
	Acrostic Poetry with Kindness	1, 3, 4, 5, 9	4, 5, 6, 11, 12
	E-Kindness Card	1, 3, 4, 7, 8, 9	4, 5, 6, 8, 11, 12
	Writing to the Author	1, 2, 3, 4, 5, 6, 7, 8, 9	4, 5, 6, 7, 8, 11, 12
	Let's Dance	1, 2, 6, 7, 8, 9	3, 4, 5, 6, 7, 8, 11, 12
	Book Review	1, 2, 3, 5, 8	4, 5, 6, 8, 11, 12
	Kindness Buttons	3, 4, 5	4, 5, 6, 11, 12
Blackberries in the Dark	Packing Your Bags	3, 5, 9	4, 8, 11, 12
	Family Traditions	4, 9	4, 5, 6, 11, 12
	Character Map	2, 3, 5	1, 2, 3, 12
	Postcard Connection	2, 3, 5	1, 2, 3, 4, 5, 6, 12
	Bedtime Stories	5, 9	1, 2, 3, 4, 8, 10, 11 12
	Rewriting the Plot	2, 3, 4, 5	1, 2, 4, 5, 6, 11, 12
	Blackberry Jam/Writing Connection	2, 3, 9	4, 5, 6, 11, 12
Everett Anderson's Goodbye	Concept Map	4, 5, 9	11, 12
	Picture Walk	4, 5	1, 3, 11, 12

Book Selection	Activity	Information Literacy Standards for Student Learning	NCTE/IRA Standards for English Language Arts
	RIVET Vocabulary Lesson	2, 4, 5, 9	11, 12
	Concept Map	4, 5, 9	11, 12
	Schema Activation	2, 3, 4, 5, 9	4, 11, 12
	Vocabulary Lesson: Word Family Word Sort	3, 5, 9	11, 12
The Fall of Freddy the Leaf	Listening Lesson	3, 5, 9	1, 4, 9, 11, 12
	Discussion Starter	5, 9	7, 8, 11, 12
	Checking for Comprehension: Discussion Questions	4, 5, 7, 9	1, 3, 4, 11, 12
	Autumn Haiku	4, 5, 6	4, 5, 6, 9, 11, 12
	Construct a Life Size Tree/ Sentence Writing	5, 6, 9	4, 5, 6, 11, 12
	Story Frame	6, 7	1, 3, 4, 6, 11, 12
Badger's Parting Gifts	Special Gifts	3, 4, 5, 9	11, 12
	Checking for Comprehension: Discussion Questions	4, 5, 7, 9	1, 3, 4, 11, 12
	Feelings	2, 3, 4, 5	1, 3, 4, 11, 12
	Tea Party Strategy	2, 3, 4, 5	1, 3, 4, 11, 12
	I Remember Poem	3, 4, 5, 9	4, 5, 6, 11, 12
	Letter Writing	3, 4, 5	4, 5, 6, 11, 12
I Had a Friend Named Peter	Think, Pair, Share	4, 5	4, 11, 12
	Checking for Comprehension: Discussion Questions	4, 5, 7, 9	1, 3, 4, 11, 12
	Open Mind Portraits	2, 3, 4, 5	1, 4, 11, 12
	All About Books	4, 5, 9	4, 5, 6, 9, 11, 12
	Prereading/KWL	2, 3, 4, 5	4, 11, 12
Sadako and the Thousand Paper Cranes	Prereading/KWL	2, 3, 4, 5	4, 11, 12
	Good Luck Charms	2, 4, 5	4, 11, 12
	Family Tree	3, 5	1, 3, 4, 11, 12
	Vocabulary Development	3, 5, 9	11, 12
	Myth Discussion	4, 5, 7, 9	1, 3, 4, 11, 12
	Paper Cranes	1, 2, 3, 4, 5	4, 8, 9, 11, 12
	Picture Frames	3, 4	11, 12
Dog Heaven	Predictions from Reading	1, 2, 6, 9	3, 4, 11
	Building Schema	2, 3, 4, 5, 9	4, 5, 6, 11, 12
	Confirming Predictions	1, 2, 6, 9	3, 4, 11, 12
	Comparison	2, 3, 4, 5, 6, 9	3, 7, 11, 12
	Memorial Stepping Stones	3, 4	11, 12
I'll Always Love You	Veterinarian Visit	4, 5, 7	4, 12
	Concept Ladder	3, 5, 9	11, 12
	Dog Years	2, 3, 4, 5	11, 12
	Postcards	2, 3, 4, 5, 7, 9	4, 5, 6, 11, 12
	Storyboarding	2, 3, 4, 5	1, 3, 11, 12
	Memory Books	1, 2, 3, 4, 5	4, 5, 6, 8, 11, 12
The Tenth Good Thing About Barney	Life Cycle	3, 4	4, 11, 12
	Vocabulary Development	3, 5, 9	11, 12
	Three-Minute Pause	2, 3, 4, 5	1, 3, 4, 11, 12
	Ten Good Things	2, 3, 4, 5, 9	3, 4, 5, 11, 12

Book Selection	Activity	Information Literacy Standards for Student Learning	NCTE/IRA Standards for English Language Arts
	Language Experience Approach	2, 3, 4, 5, 9	3, 4, 11, 12
	Bereavement Boxes	3, 4, 5	4, 11, 12
Tell Me Again About The Night I Was Born	Vocabulary Builder	1, 3, 4, 9	1, 3, 4, 5, 8, 11, 12
	Concept Mapping	4, 5, 9	11, 12
	Family Connection	3, 4, 5	4, 9, 11, 12
	Revision/Revisiting the Concept Map	4, 5, 9	1, 11, 12
	Checking for Comprehension: Discussion Questions	4, 5, 7, 9	1, 3, 4, 11, 12
	Skill Builder: Similes	3, 6, 9	3, 4, 5, 6, 11, 12
	Family Storybooks	1, 2, 3, 4, 6, 9	1, 3, 4, 5, 6, 7, 11, 12
	Diorama	1, 3, 4, 5, 6, 9	1, 3, 4, 5, 6, 11, 12
Stellaluna	KWL	1, 2, 3, 4, 5, 6, 9	1, 3, 4, 7, 11, 12
	Real Life Adoption/Mentoring	1, 9	4, 5, 6, 11, 12
	Checking for Comprehension: Discussion Questions	4, 5, 7, 9	1, 3, 4, 11, 12
	Venn Diagrams	1, 2, 3, 9	1, 3, 4, 5, 7, 11, 12
	Skill Builder: Making Words/ Building Words	1, 3, 9	1, 6, 11, 12
	Bat Mobile/Library Research	1, 2, 3, 4, 5, 6, 7, 8, 9	1, 3, 4, 5, 6, 7, 8, 11, 12
I Love You Like Crazy Cakes	Prediction	1, 2, 6, 9	3, 4, 11, 12
	Reading Comprehension/ Making Connections	3, 6, 9	1, 3, 11, 12
	Route to China	1, 2, 3, 4, 5, 8, 9	1, 3, 4, 5, 6, 7, 8, 11, 12
	Recipe for Crazy Cakes	3, 5, 9	4, 5, 6, 11, 12
	Acrostic Poem Quilt	3, 5, 9	4, 5, 6, 11, 12
	Make a Passport	3, 5, 9	4, 5, 6, 11, 12
	First Person Narrative	2, 3, 4	4, 5, 6, 11, 12
The Days of Summer	Library Skills	1, 6, 9	1, 3, 11, 12
	Concept Mapping	4, 5, 9	11, 12
	Reading Comprehension/ Making Connections	3, 6, 9	1, 3, 11, 12
	Hidden Message	1, 3, 6	1, 3, 4, 5, 6, 11, 12
Two Homes	Home Drawing Story/Letter- Sound Recognition	1, 2, 6, 9	3, 11, 12
	Building Schema	1, 2, 3, 6	1, 3, 11, 12
	Story Elements	1, 2, 3, 4, 5, 6	1, 3, 4, 11, 12
	Human Go Fish	1, 2, 3, 6, 9	3, 6, 11, 12
I Don't Want To Talk About It: Story About Divorce for Young Children	Before We Read	1, 2, 6, 9	3, 6, 11, 12
	Adopt an Animal	2, 3, 4	4, 5, 6, 11, 12
	Animal Facts	1, 2, 3, 6, 8	1, 4, 5, 6, 7, 8, 11, 12
	Similes	3, 5	4, 6, 11, 12
	Using Adjectives/Alphabetical Order	3, 5	4, 6, 11, 12
	Caboose	1, 3, 9	4, 6, 11, 12
	Using Story Words	1, 3, 9	4, 6, 11, 12
	Writing Sentences with Contractions	1, 2, 3, 6	4, 5, 6, 11, 12
	Online Zoo Visit	1, 2, 3, 6, 8	4, 5, 6, 7, 8, 11, 12
	Synonyms and Antonyms	1, 3	4, 6, 11, 12

Information Literacy Standards for Student Learning

Information Literacy

Standard 1: The student who is information literate accesses information efficiently and effectively.

Standard 2: The student who is information literate evaluates information critically and competently.

Standard 3: The student who is information literate uses information accurately and creatively.

Independent Learning

Standard 4: The student who is an independent learner is information literate and pursues information related to personal interests.

Standard 5: The student who is an independent learner is information literate and appreciates literature and other creative expressions of information.

Standard 6: The student who is an independent learner is information literate and strives for excellence in information seeking and knowledge generation.

Social Responsibility

Standard 7: The student who contributes positively to the learning community and to society is information literate and recognizes the importance of information to a democratic society.

Standard 8: The student who contributes positively to the learning community and to society is information literate and practices ethical behavior in regard to information and information technology.

Standard 9: The student who contributes positively to the learning community and to society is information literate and participates effectively in groups to pursue and generate information.

The American Library Association and the Association for Educational Communications and Technology. Copyright 1998. Reprinted by permission from the American Library Association.

NCTE/IRA Standards for English Language Arts

1. Students read a wide range of print and non-print texts to build an understanding of texts, of themselves, and of the cultures of the United States and the world; to acquire new information; to respond to the needs and demands of society and the workplace; and for personal fulfillment. Among these texts are fiction and nonfiction, classic and contemporary works.

2. Students read a wide range of literature from many periods in many genres to build an understanding of the many dimensions (e.g., philosophical, ethical, aesthetic) of human experience.

3. Students apply a wide range of strategies to comprehend, interpret, evaluate, and appreciate texts. They draw on their prior experience, their interactions with other readers and writers, their knowledge of word meaning and of other texts, their word identification strategies, and their understanding of textual features (e.g., sound-letter correspondence, sentence structure, context, graphics).

4. Students adjust their use of spoken, written, and visual language (e.g., conventions, style, vocabulary) to communicate effectively with a variety of audiences and for different purposes.

5. Students employ a wide range of strategies as they write and use different writing process elements appropriately to communicate with different audiences for a variety of purposes.

6. Students apply knowledge of language structure, language conventions (e.g., spelling and punctuation), media techniques, figurative language, and genre to create, critique, and discuss print and non-print texts.

7. Students conduct research on issues and interests by generating ideas and questions, and by posing problems. They gather, evaluate, and synthesize data from a variety of sources (e.g., print and non-print texts, artifacts, people) to communicate their discoveries in ways that suit their purpose and audience.

8. Students use a variety of technological and information resources (e.g., libraries, databases, computer networks, video) to gather and synthesize information and to create and communicate knowledge.

9. Students develop an understanding of and respect for diversity in language use, patterns, and dialects across cultures, ethnic groups, geographic regions, and social roles.

10. Students whose first language is not English make use of their first language to develop competency in the English language arts and to develop understanding of content across the curriculum.

11. Students participate as knowledgeable, reflective, creative, and critical members of a variety of literacy communities.

12. Students use spoken, written, and visual language to accomplish their own purposes (e.g., for learning, enjoyment, persuasion, and the exchange of information).

Standards for the English Language Arts, by International Reading Association and the National Council of Teachers of English, Copyright 1996 by the International Reading Association and the National Council of Teachers of English. Reprinted with permission.

Chapter 1

Bullying

Hooway for Wodney Wat

Copyright date: 1999
Author: Helen Lester
Recommended age range: five to eight

Discovery and Discussion: Setting the Stage for Reading

Summary

Rodney can't pronounce his name but becomes the class hero when he stands up to Camilla Capybara, the class bully.

- **Words for Review:** shy, bully, rodent, teasing, trampled, speech impediment

- **Being Different/Simon Says**

In the story Rodney is teased because he has a speech impediment that makes him unique and different from the other animals in school. While playing a game of Simon Says, Rodney outsmarts the class bully.

Play a variation of Simon Says with students highlighting students' unique qualities such as hair or eye color. Instruct students to pay special attention to what is being said and require them to share one unique quality they learned about their classmates at the conclusion of the game. Ask questions that highlight their differences by stating, "Simon Says everyone with blue eyes stand up, Simon Says everyone who rides a bus to school put their hand on their head, Simon Says everyone who has a cat as a pet stand on one foot." Continue this game until everyone has been included in some way. Choose questions that are appropriate for your particular group of students. At the end of the game, ask students to share something they had in common with a classmate. Then, ask students to share something unique about a classmate or themselves. Make a class list of unique qualities called "What Makes Our Class Special." This list can be used as a bulletin board or hallway display. A discussion about being unique can develop a positive self-image and self-reliance.

■ The Letter R Scavenger Hunt

Information Literacy Standards: 3, 4, 6, 9
NCTE/IRA Standards for English Language Arts: 1, 4, 5, 11, 12

Rodney has trouble pronouncing words that begin with the letter r. For younger students, this lesson can provide an opportunity to teach letter-sound correspondence. Write the letter r on the board or a transparency and ask students to draw the letter in the air as you explain how it is written. Then ask students to go on a "Letter R Scavenger Hunt" and identify anything that starts with /r/. Construct a "Letter R Journal" for each student in the following manner: 1) cut plain construction paper into fourths; 2) punch holes on left side; 3) bind with string. Students can also look through magazines and cut out words or pictures with the letter r and glue the words or pictures into their journals. Conclude by creating a class list of all the words or pictures collected by students.

■ Animal Identification

Information Literacy Standards: 1, 2, 3, 4, 6, 8, 9
NCTE/IRA Standards for English Language Arts: 1, 3, 4, 5, 6, 7, 8, 11, 12

Many different rodents are introduced in the text. For some students this may be their first exposure to animals such as: guinea pig, rat, hamster, mouse, and capybara. Review or introduce dictionary skills by modeling for students how to find the word *rodent* and the definition in the dictionary. Introduce students to these animals by showing pictures and talking about the characteristics of each. The librarian/school library media specialist can make a display of animal books from which students can browse. The librarian/school library media specialist can also direct students to the section of the library where the books on animals are shelved. Adapt for older students by using the Internet to research different rodents. Divide students into five groups and ask them to conduct research and present their findings to the class. This research will familiarize students with the characters they will meet in the story.

Exploration: During Reading

■ Reinforcement of the Letter R

Information Literacy Standards: 4, 5, 6, 9
NCTE/IRA Standards for English Language Arts: 1, 3, 11, 12

Read the book aloud without stopping. Then, reread the text and ask students to clap each time they hear /r/. This will allow for informal assessment of students' ability to recognize the letter-sound correspondence while students practice identification of that sound.

■ Feelings Chart

Information Literacy Standards: 1, 2, 5, 6, 9
NCTE/IRA Standards for English Language Arts: 1, 3, 4, 11, 12

While reading the text, have students complete a Feelings Chart found in Figure 1.1 on page 4. Each time students meet a new character in the text have students complete the following information on the Feelings Chart: 1) character's name; 2) what happened in the story; 3) character's behavior and feelings; and 4) students' own feelings about what happened. Creating this chart can assist students by connecting with the feelings of the characters in the book. For younger students, make a class list. As the students identify the information, record the information on the class list.

Reading Between the Lines: Post Reading

■ Animal Alliteration Book

Information Literacy Standards: 1, 3, 4, 5, 9
NCTE/IRA Standards for English Language Arts: 4, 5, 6, 11, 12

Alliteration is the repetition of the same initial sound in several words of a sentence. Alliteration appears in all the characters' names: Hairy Hamster, Minifeet Mouse, Grizzlefriz Guinea Pig, Camilla Capybara, and Wodney Wat. Each student picks the animal of their choice and creates a name that begins with the same letter as the animal. For example, if the student chooses the animal cat, the new name may be Chatty Cat. The word can be an adjective to describe the animal. The students then write a sentence using alliteration where each word in the sentence begins with the same letter. Then ask students to illustrate their sentence. Collect all animal alliterations and bind together with string to make a class book or simply display on a bulletin board entitled "Animal Alliteration." For younger students, create Animal Alliteration sentences as a whole group.

■ Revisiting the Text/Comprehension Questions

Information Literacy Standards: 1, 2, 3, 6, 9
NCTE/IRA Standards for English Language Arts: 1, 3, 4, 11, 12

Reread the text and ask the following questions:
Page 5
1. What is Rodney's problem at the beginning of the story?
2. Explain why this problem makes him unique.
3. Predict what might happen to Rodney.

Preview the illustration on page 7
4. Explain what is happening in this illustration.
5. How might Rodney feel?

Pages 8-9
6. Describe Rodney's behavior.

Pages 10-15
7. What is a bully?
8. Who is Camilla Capybara?
9. Describe Camilla Capybara.
10. How does she make the other rodents feel? How do you know? Why might she be considered a bully?

Feelings Chart

Character's Name

What's happening?

Character's behavior and feelings

My feelings

Character's Name

What's happening?

Character's behavior and feelings

My feelings

Character's Name

What's happening?

Character's behavior and feelings

My feelings

Feelings Chart. Figure 1.1

Pages 16-24

11. What does Camilla do that makes the other rodents laugh?

Pages 25-32

12. What eventually happens to Camilla?

13. Why is Rodney considered a hero to his classmates?

14. Do you consider Rodney to be a hero? Why/Why not?

Beyond the Text: Lesson Extensions

■ Anti-Bullying Poster

Information Literacy Standards: 1, 3, 4, 5, 6, 7, 9
NCTE/IRA Standards for English Language Arts: 1, 4, 5, 6, 7, 11, 12

Rodney is bullied by many of his classmates. Ask students to brainstorm what it means to be bullied. Also discuss with students what it means to be a bully. Students can share stories that illustrate either being bullied or being a bully. Emphasize how this type of behavior cannot be tolerated in school. Ask students to create a list of ways to help stop bullying in their school. Divide students into manageable groups to create an anti-bullying poster to promote appropriate behavior. Students can work together to create an anti-bullying slogan for their posters.

Have students sign an anti-bullying pledge or create a class pledge of your own. Dr. Phil's anti-bullying pledge can be found at: <www.menstuff.org/issues/byissue/bullying.html#students>

■ Bully Box

Information Literacy Standards: 1, 2, 4, 5, 6, 7, 9
NCTE/IRA Standards for English Language Arts: 1, 3, 4, 7, 11, 12

Decorate a shoebox and label it "Bully Box." On strips of paper write examples of different scenarios where students are being bullied and place in box. Older students can brainstorm scenarios to place in the box. For confidentiality reasons, instruct students not to write their names on the entries. Pick a situation from the Bully Box and read it aloud to students. This activity helps students' develop empathy. Ask students the following questions:

1. How can you identify the bully in this scenario? What is happening that helps you identify the bully?

2. Who is being bullied in this scenario? How do you know? What actions help you come to that decision?

3. How do you think this person feels?

4. How would you feel if this were you?

5. Why might the bully be doing this?

6. What would you do if you were the person being bullied?

7. If you saw someone being bullied, what could you do to prevent this from happening?

The Sissy Duckling

Copyright date: 2002
Author: Harvey Fierstein
Recommended age range: five to nine

Discovery and Discussion: Setting the Stage for Reading

- **Words for Review:** hunter, flock, wounded, duckling, chided, winter, spring, bravery, ingenuity, loyalty, hero

- **Investigating Stereotypes**

Elmer is criticized because he does not like to do what the other boy ducklings like to do. Before reading *The Sissy Duckling*, investigate and discuss gender stereotypes with students. Make three headings on the board, chart paper, or a transparency: "Male," "Female," and "Both." Ask students to identify as many gender stereotypes and traditional ways of looking at gender as possible. Students may share personal experiences from home or school that identify these stereotypes. Provoke discussion by asking the following questions:

1. In what ways does the "Male" list differ from the "Female" list? If there are differences, why?

2. What do the lists have in common? Why? (if applicable)

3. Have you ever experienced a stereotype such as "You are a girl; you can't play football?" Allow students to share their experiences.

A discussion will lend itself in preparation for reading the text. Preview the title and illustration on the cover of the book. Ask students to think about what Elmer might be doing in the story that the other boy ducklings consider "sissy." Preview the illustrations on pages two, three, and four and ask the same question.

- **Musical Chairs**

Information Literacy Standards: 3, 4, 5, 6, 9
NCTE/IRA Standards for English Language Arts: 4, 5, 11, 12

Play musical chairs with the students by eliminating a chair, not a child. Students must work together to figure out what to do as a team when the music stops and there are not enough chairs for everyone. After the game, ask students to write in their journals what it felt like to be excluded from the group. What did they do to overcome the obstacle of not having enough chairs for everyone?

- **Classroom Community**

Information Literacy Standards: 6, 9
NCTE/IRA Standards for English Language Arts: 1, 6, 11, 12

Summary

Based on Harvey Fierstein's award-winning HBO special, Elmer is laughed at and teased by all the other boy ducklings in the forest. Despite the constant teasing, Elmer is a very happy duckling and continues to do what he likes best such as baking cakes. As hunting season approaches, Elmer has the opportunity to show everyone how special he really is.

Reinforce the concept of classroom community with students. Brainstorm with students what it means to belong to a community, then as a whole group, create a list of Community Rules to be posted in the classroom or library. Begin the list by writing, "Respect each other." Ask students what other rules could be included so that everyone feels like they are equally important despite their differences. This activity will reinforce tolerance of differences.

Exploration: During Reading

■ Beach Ball Comprehension

Information Literacy Standards: 1, 2, 6, 9
NCTE/IRA Standards for English Language Arts: 1, 3, 4, 11, 12

While reading the text, stop periodically and toss a beach ball to students to check for comprehension and elicit discussion. When students answer the question correctly, they are permitted to throw the ball to a classmate. In order to ensure all students have a chance, tell students that they may only have the beach ball once during the duration of the activity.

To prepare the beach ball, simply buy any size beach ball. Using a permanent marker, write comprehension questions for the text on each of the colored sections. Questions to write on the beach ball may include: 1) What is the setting of the story?; 2) Describe the main character up to this point in the story; 3) Predict what might happen next in the story; 4) What is the problem or conflict?; 5) How is the conflict resolved?

Reading Between the Lines: Post Reading

■ Dissecting a Character

Information Literacy Standards: 1, 2, 3, 4, 6, 7, 9
NCTE/IRA Standards for English Language Arts: 1, 3, 4, 11, 12

Duplicate the Character Cards provided in Figure 1.2 on page 7.

Hold up one character card to show the entire class. Briefly discuss the role that character played in the text. Make two columns on the board: label column one "outside" and column two "inside." Ask the students to brainstorm a list of words that describe the character's "outside," i.e., his appearance. Write students' suggestions in the "outside" column on the board. Do the same for their suggestions for the "inside" column. This serves as a model for what students will be required to do in their cooperative groups. When the class lists are complete, divide the students into groups with each group receiving one of the character cards, a copy of the book, a piece of large construction paper or butcher paper, and crayons or colored pencils. Instruct students to make a drawing of their character at the top of the paper. Remind students to be as detailed as possible, although their drawing will not be graded. Students then brainstorm words that describe their characters' "insides." They write those words inside their drawing. After all groups complete this activity, ask them to share with the class. This lesson can familiarize students with all the story's characters and their traits.

Character Cards

Elmer

Mama

Papa

Drake

Character Cards. Figure 1.2.

■ Readers Theater

Information Literacy Standards: 1, 2, 3, 4, 5, 6, 7, 9
NCTE/IRA Standards for English Language Arts: 1, 3, 4, 5, 6, 8, 11, 12

Readers Theater is an interactive strategy to summarize what was learned in a text. It also reinforces fluency and expressive meaningful language as students use their reading voices for performance purposes.

For younger students, write a script for students as directed below. Challenge older students to write the script together and record it or students can be challenged to write their own scripts to show their understanding of literary elements. In order to involve students in the creation of the script, each student or group of students needs a copy of the text. Revisit the text and select the dialogue the characters use. Highlighting or marking the text in some fashion to distinguish between characters and narrator can accomplish this. When the text has been dissected, the script can be written. Use the exact words of the author or adapt for your students' needs and reading abilities. Type the script and distribute a copy to each student.

Performing Readers Theater is quite simple since students are permitted to read from the script during the performance. Addition of music and sound effects, when appropriate, is a fun way for students without speaking parts to be involved. Rehearsal of the performance will improve fluency as students work on repeatedly reading the text. After students' reading becomes fluent, they can practice voice intonation and performance skills.

■ Compare/Contrast Diagram

Information Literacy Standards: 1, 2, 3, 6, 9
NCTE/IRA Standards for English Language Arts: 1, 3, 4, 11, 12

Read a variation of *The Ugly Duckling* by Hans Christian Anderson. Use the Compare/Contrast Diagram in Figure 1.3 on page 9 to find similarities and differences in *The Sissy Duckling* and any version of *The Ugly Duckling*. Students will gain the knowledge of understanding how the two texts are alike and different. For younger students, simply make a transparency of the figure or draw your own on butcher paper to complete as a whole class.

■ What Is the Consequence?

Information Literacy Standards: 1, 2, 3, 4, 6, 9
NCTE/IRA Standards for English Language Arts: 1, 3, 4, 11, 12

This activity will help students reflect on the main character's behavior as well as identify with the other characters' reasons for behaving in the manner in which they did. Using the board, chart paper, or a transparency, write four boxes horizontally as shown in Figure 1.4, What Is the Consequence?

Character	Behavior	Why?	Result

What Is the Consequence? Figure 1.4

Compare/Contrast Diagram

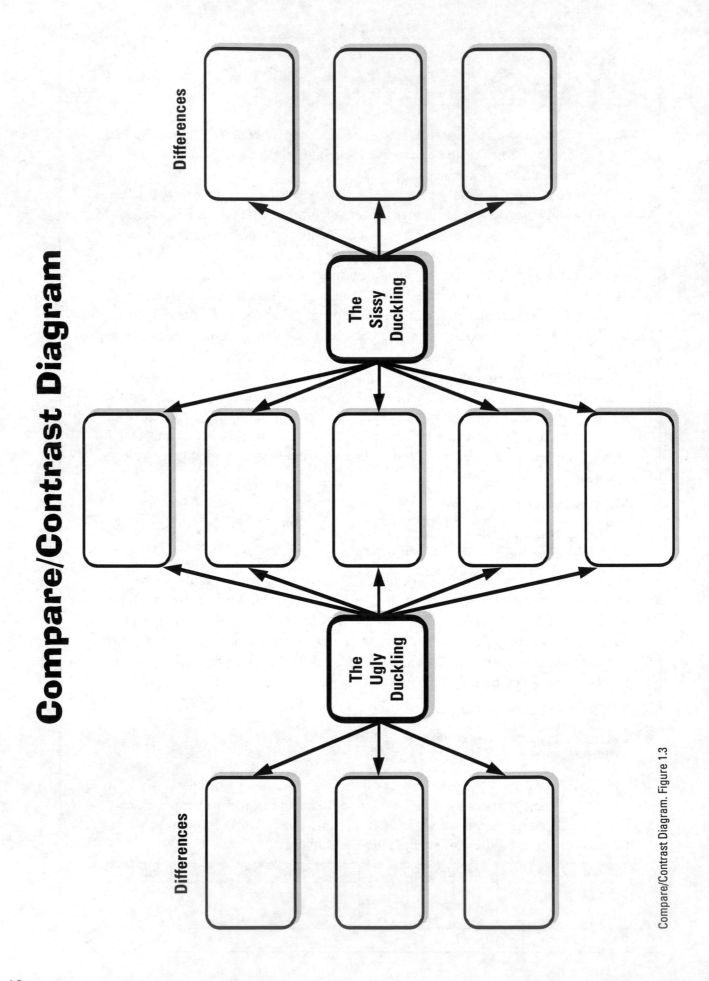

Differences

The Sissy Duckling

The Ugly Duckling

Differences

Compare/Contrast Diagram. Figure 1.3

Ask students to reflect on one of the characters in the story. Write that character's name in the box. After students have given a character's name, ask them what words might be used to describe the character's behavior in the story. Write these words in the second box. For the third box ask students why the character behaved in this fashion and write their answers in the third box. To complete the fourth box, ask students to brainstorm the result of these actions. Continue this process until all the major characters are discussed from the text. For younger students or students struggling with this activity, model a Think Aloud to illustrate how to respond in each of the four categories.

Beyond the Text: Lesson Extensions

■ Working with Onsets and Rimes

Information Literacy Standards: 1, 7, 9
NCTE/IRA Standards for English Language Arts: 4, 6, 11, 12

Onsets and rimes are parts of spoken language that are syllables. An onset is the initial consonant(s) sound of a syllable (the onset of bag is b-; of swim, is sw-). A rime is the part of the syllable that contains the vowel and all that follows (the rime of bag is –ag; of swim, -im). Not all syllables or words have an onset, but they all have a rime (e.g., the word or syllable "out" is a rime without an onset).This strategy, appropriate for whole group or small group instruction, can be used to reinforce the skill of identifying onsets and rimes and to help students think about word families/patterns. Each student or team is given a Working with Onsets and Rimes Sheet shown in Figure 1.6 on page 12. Along the top row, choose five word patterns from the text such as the rimes "it" or "at." Down the left hand side, provide a random set of onsets in the form of consonants or consonant blends. Words from the text should be of central focus. An example is provided below in Figure 1.5.

	it	at	ick	in
p	pit			pin
m				
ch				
f				

Working with Onsets and Rimes Example. Figure 1.5

Challenge students to think of as many words as possible for each combination. Award points to the student or team that creates the most words. Emphasize that nonsense words are unacceptable and no points will be awarded.

Working with Onsets and Rimes

Directions: Complete this table as directed.

Working with Onsets and Rimes Sheet. Figure 1.6

■ Making Words

Information Literacy Standards: 1, 7, 9
NCTE/IRA Standards for English Language Arts: 4, 6, 11, 12

Write the title of the book, *The Sissy Duckling*, on the board or a transparency. Challenge students to create as many words from the book's title as possible. Record the words on the board or a transparency. Divide the class into teams of four or five and appoint a secretary. Each team brainstorms as many words as possible without adding any additional letters or repeating letters. Instruct students to check the dictionary if necessary. Only the letters on the board or the transparency can be used. Be sure to point out to students that sometimes there are words within words such as the word duck in duckling. Choose an appropriate time limit. When time has passed, ask each team to present their word lists, make a class word list and hang it up to be used as a word wall.

■ Egg Hero Descriptive Writing (grades two and up)

Information Literacy Standards: 1, 3, 4, 5, 9
NCTE/IRA Standards for English Language Arts: 4, 5, 6, 11, 12

Review the definition of an adjective. Ask students to think of their hero and write a list of ten adjectives to describe that person. Remind students to think of words that describe their personality and not their appearance. Examples of adjectives might include: brave, courageous, or strong. When students have their list completed, they can then create that person using an uncooked or plastic egg. Ask each student to bring in an egg with the middle blown out or provide a plastic egg for each student. Poking a hole in each end of the egg (uncooked) with a nail or screw and blowing the middle from it can accomplish this. The egg will then be a shell. For plastic eggs, no preparation is needed. Ask students to decorate the egg to resemble their hero. They can use yarn for hair, draw a face with pencil or marker, use sequins for eyes, or use clay for molding a nose or ears. The possibilities are endless. After students have created their hero, they are to use the ten adjectives from their list to write a descriptive paragraph about their hero. They must emphasize the adjectives they have chosen. Students can type their paragraphs and mount the essay on tag board or construction paper. Students can share their egg and paragraph before displaying them in the hallway display case or on a bookshelf for others to enjoy.

■ Write a Book Review

Information Literacy Standards: 1, 2, 3, 5, 8
NCTE/IRA Standards for English Language Arts: 4, 5, 6, 8, 11, 12

Students can write a book review and post it on the Internet at <www.rif.org/ readingplanet/bookzone/> or write a whole class review and post it on the Web site. This may be a teachable moment on advising students about best practices when posting information on the Internet. Review policies for posting on the Web. Posting the review to the library's Web site is another option.

Goggles

Copyright date: 1998
Author: Ezra Jack Keats
Recommended age range: five to eight
Award: Caldecott Honor Book

Discovery and Discussion: Setting the Stage for Reading

Summary

Peter and Archie must deal with the neighborhood bullies who attempt to take possession of their newly found prize possession, a pair of motorcycle goggles. Peter's dog, Willie, along with the boys' quick wit, comes to the rescue. This book is a multicultural selection.

■ **Words for Review:** goggle, hideout, snatched, gasped

■ **Preparing to Read**

Information Literacy Standards: 2, 3, 7, 9
NCTE/IRA Standards for English Language Arts: 4, 11, 12

Hold up the book. Ask students: 1) to read the title and author; 2) to define the word "goggles;" 3) to identify the objects on the cover's illustration; and 4) to make predictions about the story's setting, plot, and characters. Write students' predictions on the board or chart paper. Revisit the predictions after the text is read to confirm or revise.

■ **Prereading Questions**

Information Literacy Standards: 2, 3, 7, 9
NCTE/IRA Standards for English Language Arts: 4, 11, 12

Ask students the following questions:

1. Have you ever found something that someone lost?
2. What did you do with the item?
3. What should you do with an item that you find?
4. When you are afraid, how do you feel?
5. Ask students to explain their feelings when they are afraid of someone or something.

Make a class list to refer to during reading. Periodically, compare how Peter and Archie feel during different parts of the story.

Exploration: During Reading

■ **Story Imaging**

Information Literacy Standards: 1, 3, 6
NCTE/IRA Standards for English Language Arts: 1, 3, 11, 12

Stop reading and ask students to close their eyes and "see" the characters, setting, and events in the story. Ask students to recall the first event of the story they heard (or read). Ask them to raise their hand when they have the picture in their minds. When all hands are raised, ask students to tell the class what they visualized and encourage them to give as much detail as possible. Stop throughout the story and do the same again. At the end of the story, assign students to small groups. Give each group a piece of white paper folded into six equal panels to create a storyboard. The group then chooses six events that they have visualized to draw in sequence. Students take turns retelling the story using the storyboard from the group. The Story Imaging Checklist in Figure 1.7 on page 16 may be used as an assessment tool.

■ Flannel Board

Information Literacy Standards: 1, 2, 3, 6
NCTE/IRA Standards for English Language Arts: 1, 2, 4, 11, 12

Make a flannel board to tell the story as you read. Use "pollen" or "interfacing" (available at any craft store) and trace the characters from the text. Cover a project board with felt and the figures will stick to the board. While reading a portion of the book, stop and ask students to "show" what happened by using the felt characters.

Reading Between the Lines: Post Reading

■ Book Boxes

Information Literacy Standards: 1, 2, 3, 4, 5, 9
NCTE/IRA Standards for English Language Arts: 1, 3, 4, 5, 6, 7, 11, 12

After reading *Goggles,* make a class list of important objects in the story. Decorate a shoebox or some type of container with the title of the book and other important words from the text to show as a model for students. Ask students to do the same at home by decorating their own box for the book. Instruct students to place three to five objects or pictures in the box with an explanation as to their importance in the story. Share completed boxes in class. As an alternative, you can create a book box prior to reading to introduce the book and spark interest in the text.

■ Checking for Comprehension: Discussion Questions

Information Literacy Standards: 4, 5, 7, 9
NCTE/IRA Standards for English Language Arts: 1, 3, 4, 11, 12

Setting
Ask students the following questions:
1. Where did the story take place?
2. How did the author tell you where the story was happening?
3. Why do you think the author had the story take place in this particular setting?
4. How would the story change if the setting were different?

Resolution
Ask students the following questions:
1. How was the problem resolved in the story?
2. Is that the way you would have solved the problem?
3. What is another way Peter and Archie might have solved the problem?

Story Imaging Checklist

Story Element	Yes	No
Beginning of story		
Middle of story		
End of story		
Setting		
Characters		
Conflict/Problem		
Resolution		

Story Imaging Checklist. Figure 1.7

■ Bumper Sticker

Information Literacy Standards: 1, 3, 4, 6, 9
NCTE/IRA Standards for English Language Arts: 4, 5, 6, 11, 12

Discuss with students the purpose of a bumper sticker (relay a message, make a statement). Direct students to think of a universal message based on the anti-bullying theme that would be appropriate to place on a car bumper for others to read. This activity can be done on paper or on the computer using the word processor. Have students share their bumper stickers with the class. Display the bumper stickers around the library or classroom.

■ Character Comparison/Contrast

Information Literacy Standards: 1, 2, 3, 6
NCTE/IRA Standards for English Language Arts: 1, 3, 4, 11, 12

Using Figure 1.8 on page 18, Character Comparison/Contrast, have students create a chart to share with the class that compares similarities and contrasts differences in Peter, Archie, and the neighborhood bullies.

Beyond the Text: Lesson Extensions

■ Egg Carton Goggles

Gather paper egg cartons, pipe cleaners, tempera paint, and brushes for students to make their own pair of goggles. Cut two individual egg carton sections to be used as the goggles. Cut the tips off of the bottom to make a hole large enough to see. Attach the goggle pieces together with a pipe cleaner and use two additional pipe cleaners to be used as earpieces. Bend the pipe cleaners to fit over the students' ears. Students can paint their goggles any color. Let goggles dry thoroughly before wearing.

■ Developing Dialogue

Information Literacy Standards: 1, 2, 3, 4, 5, 6, 9
NCTE/IRA Standards for English Language Arts: 1, 3, 4, 5, 6, 11, 12

Look at the example of dialogue on the last page of the text. Explain to students that dialogue is when a character speaks. Quotation marks are used to indicate that someone is speaking. Read the page to students and ask them to think of other things that Archie and Peter could have said. Ask students to rewrite the dialogue for the last page of the text. Show students where the quotation marks and punctuation are placed. For younger students, conduct this activity as a whole class.

■ Repetitive Pattern/Spelling Rules (grades two and up)

Many words ending in "ed" are used throughout the story to signify past tense. Explain the suffix "ed" rule concerning doubling letters. Use each word in a sentence.

■ Book Jacket Design (grades two and up)

Information Literacy Standards: 1, 2, 3, 4, 5, 6, 9
NCTE/IRA Standards for English Language Arts: 1, 3, 4, 5, 6, 11, 12

Character Comparison/Contrast

Directions: Write a complete sentence to describe how the characters are alike in the first block labeled "How are these characters alike?" Write a complete sentence to describe how the characters are different in the second block labeled "How are these characters different?"

Peter	Archie	Bullies

How are these characters alike?

How are these characters different?

Character Comparison/Contrast. Figure 1.8

After carefully reviewing the components of a book jacket that may include author, title, illustrator, and author's biography, and other books by the author, have students design a book jacket for *Goggles*. Students can include a summary of the book, quotations from reviewers and even a photograph of the author, either real or imagined.

Additional Book Selections, Professional Resources, and Web Connections on Bullying

Aliki. *A Play's the Thing*. Harper Collins, 2005. Ages six-nine.
> Jose, a troublemaker and bully, creates problems when his class puts on a play. The play itself deals with a bully, who, by the end, learns to get along with others. Jose learns a lesson from the play.

Bang, Majorie. *When Sophie Get Angry...Really Really Angry*. Scholastic, 2004. Ages four-seven.
> A young girl is upset and does not know how to manage her anger but takes the time to cool off and regain her composure. Caldecott Honor Book.

Best, Cari. *Shrinking Violet*. Farrar, Straus, Giroux, 2001. Ages five-eight.
> Violet, a shy child finds the gumption to withstand a bully's taunts and saves the school from disaster. Award winning author.

Blume, Judy. *Blubber*. Yearling, 1976. Ages nine-twelve.
> Jill goes along with the rest of the fifth-grade class in tormenting a classmate and then finds out what it is like when she, too, becomes a target. Award winning author.

Bunting, Eve. *Your Move*. Harcourt Children's Books, 1998. Ages five-eight.
> When ten-year-old James' gang initiation endangers his six-year-old brother Isaac, they find the courage to say, "Thanks, but no thanks." A multicultural selection. Caldecott Award winning author.

Burnett, Karen Gedig. *Simon's Hook: A Story About Teases and Put Downs*. GR Publishing, 2000. Ages six-nine.
> Children learn several ways to deal with teasing, from ignoring the teaser to changing the subject to avoiding situations. The National Parenting Center's Seal of Approval Award.

Calahan, Tara and Derek Munson. *Enemy Pie*. Chronicle, 2000. Ages five-eight.
> Hoping that the enemy pie that his father makes will help him get rid of his enemy, a little boy finds that instead it helps him make a new friend. Children's Choice Book Award Nominee, Children's Choices Picture Book Award Nomination. Reading Rainbow Book.

Choi, Yangsook. *The Name Jar*. Dragonfly, 2003. Ages five-eight.
> Because of her Korean name, Unhei is teased by the children on the bus. Award winning author. A multicultural selection.

De Pino, Catherine. *Blue Cheese Breath and Stinky Feet: How to Deal with Bullies.* American Psychological Association, 2004. Ages six-twelve.

> With the help of his teacher and his parents, Steve devises "The Plan," strategies for avoiding, defending against, and disarming a bully who has been tormenting him at school.

Duffey, Betsy. *How to Be Cool in the Third Grade.* Puffin Books, 1993. Ages nine-twelve.

> When a bully at school marks Robbie York as a target, he decides that the only way to survive the third grade is by being cool.

Estes, Eleanor. *The Hundred Dresses.* Harcourt, 2004. Ages eight-eleven.

> In winning a medal she is no longer there to receive, a tight-lipped little Polish girl teaches her classmates a lesson. Newbery Honor Book.

Gammell, Stephen. *Twigboy.* Harcourt, 2000. Ages five-seven.

> Rockwell, a rolling rock, saves Twigboy from being bullied, and together the two set out to get revenge.

Howe, James. *Pinky and Rex and the Bully.* Spotlight, 2006. Ages six-nine.

> Pinky learns the importance of identity as he defends his favorite color, pink, and his friendship with a girl, Rex, from the neighborhood bully.

Jian, Ji-Li & David H. Hwang. *Red Scarf Girl: A Memoir of the Cultural Revolution.* HarperTrophy, 1998. Ages nine-twelve.

> True story of the author's life torn apart by the Cultural Revolution. Terror surrounds her as her favorite teachers are harassed at school, people's homes are ransacked, and her father is humiliated. A multicultural selection.

Johnson, D. B. *Eddie's Kingdom.* Houghton Mifflin, 2005. Ages six-eight.

> His neighbors who live in his apartment building, Peaceable Building, bully Eddie. He finds a resourceful way of dealing with his neighbors who blamed Eddie for all their problems. Award winning author. Boston Globe-Horn Book Award.

Joosse, Barbara M. *Stars in the Darkness.* Chronicle, 2001. Ages five-seven.

> A small boy joins with his mother to find a creative way to save his older brother from the dangers of gang violence. Includes a list of organizations and Web sites dealing with gang prevention. A multicultural selection. *New York Times* Best Illustrated Children's Books Award, Bookbuilders West Certificate of Excellence Award, and Bookbuilders West "Best of the West" Award.

Levert, Mireille. *Eddie Longpants.* Groundwood, 2005. Ages six-eight.

> Eddie is taller than other children in his class and becomes the victim of name-calling by the class bully, Peter.

McCain, Becky Ray. *Nobody Knew What to Do: A Story About Bullying.* A. Whitman, 2001. Ages five-eight.

> When bullies pick on a boy at school, a classmate is afraid, but decides that he must do something.

Naylor, Phyllis Reynolds. *The King of the Playground.* Aladdin, 1994. Ages five-eight.

> With his dad's help, Kevin overcomes his fear of the "King of the Playground" who has threatened to tie him to the slide, put him in a deep hole, or put him in a cage with bears. Newbery Award winning author.

Nickle, John. *The Ant Bully.* Scholastic, 2006. Ages five-eight.
Lucas learns a lesson about bullying when he is pulled into the ant hole he has been tormenting.

Nixon, Joan Lowery. *Caught in the Act.* Laurel Leaf, 1996. Ages nine-twelve.
Eleven-year-old Michael Patrick Kelly from New York City is sent to a foster home, a Missouri farm with a sadistic owner, a bullying son, and a number of secrets, one of which may be murder.

Olivas, Daniel A. *Benjamin and the Word/Benjamin y la palabra.* Piñata, 2005. Ages six-nine.
A bilingual book in which a Hispanic boy, Benjamin, beats his friend, James, in a game of handball, which results in a name-calling battle. Benjamin's father helps resolve the conflict. A multicultural selection.

O'Neil, Alexis. *The Recess Queen.* Scholastic, 2002. Ages five-eight.
Mean Jean is the biggest bully on the school playground until a new girl arrives and challenges Jean's status as the Recess Queen.

Oppenheim, Shulamith L. *Yanni Rubbish.* Boyds Mills Press, 2005. Ages five-eight.
The other boys, who nickname him "Yanni Rubbish," cruelly taunt Yanni and his donkey but he and his mother eventually come up with an inspired solution to deal with the problem. A multicultural selection.

Rodriguez, Luis J. *It Doesn't Have to Be This Way: A Barrio Story/No Tiene Que Ser Asi.* Childrens' Book Press, 1999. Ages five-eight.
Reluctantly, a young boy becomes more and more involved in the activities of a local gang, until a tragic event involving his cousin forces him to make a choice about the course of his life. A multicultural selection.

Stevens, Janet and Susan Crummel. *The Great Fuzz Frenzy.* Harcourt, 2005. Ages six-eight.
Big Bark, the local bully, tries to take over Dog Violet's tennis ball and the feud begins. Pip Squeak comes to the rescue. Caldecott Award winning author.

Van Draanen, Wendelin. *Shredder-Man: Secret Identity.* Random House, 2006. Ages seven-ten.
Nolan Byrd, the "nerd" suffers at the hands of school bully, Bubba Bixby until Nolan creates cyber superhero, Shredder-Man. Pennsylvania School Librarians Best of the Best Children's Books Choice Award. Rhode Island Children's Book Award.

Wilhelm, Hans. *Tyrone the Horrible.* Scholastic, 2001. Ages six-eight.
A little dinosaur named Boland tries several ways of dealing with the biggest bully in the swamp forest, until finally hitting on a successful tactic.

Professional Resources

Barton, Elizabeth. *Bully Prevention Tips and Strategies for School Leaders and Classroom Teachers.* Pearson, 2003.

> This is a guide for school leaders and educators that defines the bully-victim-witness relationship and offers guidelines for identifying bullying behaviors in the classroom.

Beane, Allan A. *The Bully Free Classroom: Over 100 Tips and Strategies for Teachers K-8.* Free Spirit, 1999.

> This text discusses classroom management tips and other helpful ideas to confront bullying.

Coloroso, Barbara. *The Bully, The Bullied, and the Bystander: From Preschool to High School: How Parents and Teachers Can Help Break the Cycle of Violence.* Harper Resource, 2003.

> This resource is a groundbreaking guide to the escalating problem of bullying.

Olweus, Dan. *Bullying at School: What We Know and What We Can Do.* Blackwell, 1993.

> This is a definitive book on bully/victim problems in school and on effective ways of counteracting and preventing such problems.

Sartori, Rosanne. *Stand Up Against Bullies!* Marco, 2005.

> Using stories, role-play, and accompanying activities, children will learn 12 strategies to help them handle a bullying situation in a non-aggressive manner. Recommended for grades K-2.

Web Connections

Bully Police
<http://bullypolice.org>

> This Web site is a comprehensive site advocating for bullied children. It also contains an extensive list of resource links on everything you need to know about bullying and gives current legislation regarding anti-bullying laws as well as information on an anti-bullying award program for schools.

Don't Laugh at Me
<http://dontlaugh.org/programs.htm>

> This site provides free "Don't Laugh at Me" program bully prevention curriculum materials.

Stop Bullying Now
<http://stopbullyingnow.hrsa.gov/index.asp>

> Created by the U.S. Department of Health and Human Services, this bilingual site contains factual information for educators on bully prevention as well as Webisodes and activities that can be used in the classroom.

Chapter 2

Peer Acceptance

Elmer

Copyright date: 2004
Author: David McKee
Recommended age range: five to eight

Discovery and Discussion: Setting the Stage for Reading

- **Words for Review:** elephant, herd, patchwork, jungle

- **The Power of Laughter**
Elmer likes to play pranks to make the other elephants laugh. Discuss with students what makes them laugh. Extend the discussion to include the important lesson that laughing with someone is different from laughing at someone. Show the cover of the book. Does this evoke laughter in students? Ask students to explain their reasons.

- **Consonant Variations**

Summary

Elmer is different from the other elephants because of his patchwork and personality. He finds fitting in with the herd can be difficult at times, but his sense of humor wins the other elephants over as he learns that being unique is a quality he would like to keep.

Information Literacy Standards: 1, 2, 6, 9
NCTE/IRA Standards for English Language Arts: 6, 11, 12

Write the word *elephant* on the board underlining the "ph." Say the word aloud emphasizing the /f/ sound as you enunciate the word. Ask students to repeat the word. Next, chunk the word, el-e-ph-ant emphasizing the /f/ sound again. Require students to do the same. Explain to students that the letters *ph* can make the /f/ sound. Write additional examples on the board such as: phone, photo, phase, gopher, dolphin, and triumph. Ask students to repeat the steps above for each word. Can you hear the /ph/ or /f/ sound in each of those words?

■ I Am Unique

Information Literacy Standards: 3, 5, 9
NCTE/IRA Standards for English Language Arts: 4, 6, 11, 12

Require students to complete the sentence starter "I am unique because…" Ask students to write their sentence on a sentence strip to hang in the library or classroom. While reading the book, remind students what they wrote and relate that to the text.

■ Fitting In

Elmer tries to fit in with the herd. Ask students to think of a time they wanted to fit into a group. Discuss these examples as a whole class.

Exploration: During Reading

Elmer covers himself in elephant colored berries to "fit in" with the herd. Stop after reading page 14 and discuss how this might be similar to or different from their experiences of "fitting in."

Reading Between the Lines: Post Reading

■ Flipbook Summary (grades one and up)

Information Literacy Standards: 1, 3, 4, 9
NCTE/IRA Standards for English Language Arts: 1, 3, 4, 5, 6, 11, 12

The ability to retell the story is one way to assess comprehension of text. This activity will help students retell the story in written form emphasizing sequencing of events. This activity can be used with any story simply by making three columns on the board or a transparency labeled *beginning, middle,* and *end.* Brainstorm events that took place in the *beginning, middle* and *end* of the story. Write students' responses in the appropriate column. Show students an example of a flipbook with the title and author in the first box, event in the beginning in second box, event in the middle in the third box, event at the end in the fourth box. When students flip up the sectioned flap, they draw a corresponding picture in the space under the flap. Have students share their flipbooks with the class. Encourage variety in their work.

■ Patchwork Quilt

Information Literacy Standards: 1, 2, 3, 5, 9
NCTE/IRA Standards for English Language Arts: 1, 3, 4, 5, 6, 11, 12

Give each student a square of 4" x 4" plain white paper. Ask students to portray their favorite part of the story, either through illustration or written words. When completed, each student shares the square or quilt piece. Hang a large piece of butcher paper on the wall for students to place their quilt piece. After students present, they are permitted to add their piece to the quilt.

■ **Patchwork Jungle Animals**

Elmer is many different colors. Revisit the cover of the book and point out the different colors of his hide. Make a list on the board of other animals from the story. Revisit the book if necessary or add additional jungle animals not mentioned in the text. Distribute various colored tissue paper squares, one piece of oak tag, scissors, and glue to students. Ask students to create their own patchwork animal by using the supplies provided. They can create an elephant or any other animal from the jungle. Students draw their animal on oak tag, or use tracers if available, and cut out the figure. Then they use the squares of tissue paper to make the hide or skin of their animal. Glue the tissue paper to the animal. Exhibit on a bulletin board or create a display in the library with the heading "Patchwork Jungle Animals: We are all alike."

Beyond the Text: Lesson Extensions

■ **Writing a Sequel (grades two and up)**

Information Literacy Standards: 1, 3, 4, 6, 8, 11, 12
NCTE/IRA Standards for English Language Arts: 1, 3, 4, 5, 6, 8, 11, 12

Divide students into groups and ask them to write and illustrate the sequel to *Elmer*. Explain the concept of a sequel, a book that picks up where the first book left off. Give students some examples of sequels that may be familiar to them, such as dePaola's *Strega Nona Meets Her Match*, a sequel to *Strega Nona: Her Story*.

To assist students in writing their sequel, they must first think about how the original story ends and what adventures might Elmer experience next. When each group has an idea, distribute white drawing paper, rules, pencils, markers, crayons, magazines, glue, and other supplies to students. Let them decide how the book will be written and illustrated, but the cover should include the title, author(s), and illustrator(s). Encourage creativity and teamwork as students develop the *Elmer* sequel. Students can publish their sequel to the library's Web site or bind with string and display in the library. Students can also share their sequels orally.

■ **Share Additional Books in the Series**

David McKee has written other books about Elmer that you may want to share with students. Titles include: *Elmer's Friends, Elmer's New Friend, Elmer's Colors Board Book,* and *Elmer Takes Off.* Encourage students to check these books out of the library or put a few *Elmer* books in a backpack for students to take home over the weekend. Encourage students who take the backpack home to give a short book talk on one of the books they read when they return the backpack.

■ **Elephant Detectives (grades two and up)**

Information Literacy Standards: 1, 2, 3, 4, 6, 7, 8, 9
NCTE/IRA Standards for English Language Arts: 1, 3, 4, 5, 6, 7, 8, 11, 12

Give each student an Elephant Detective KWL (What I Know, What I Want to Know, What I Learned) (Ogle, 1986) shown in Figure 2.1 on page 26 and complete as a whole group. Based on the information gained from the second column, What I

Elephant Detective KWL

K What I Know	W What I want to Know	L What did I learn?

©2006 Inspiration Software®, Inc. Graphics created in Inspiration® Software, Inc. Used with permission.

Elephant Detective. KWL. Figure 2.1

Want to Know, students investigate elephants using the Web site <http://elephants.bizhat. com>. Divide students into manageable groups to read and document the answers to the questions generated on the KWL chart. Groups report back to the class with the information gathered. Visit the library and look for informational texts about elephants to share with the class.

Horace and Morris, but Mostly Dolores

Copyright date: 1999
Author: James Howe
Recommended age range: five to eight

Discovery and Discussion: Setting the Stage for Reading

■ **Words for Review:** adventure, sewer, decision, clubhouse, downhearted

■ **Prereading/Predicting**

> *Information Literacy Standards: 1, 2, 6, 9*
> *NCTE/IRA Standards for English Language Arts: 3, 4, 11, 12*

Brainstorm with students the definition of adventure. Ask students to share an adventure they have gone on or would like to go on one day. Show the cover of the book, *Horace and Morris, but Mostly Dolores,* and ask students to name the animals on the cover. Ask students to predict what type of adventures mice might experience. Make a class list of these predictions. After reading the text, revisit the list to confirm or revise predictions based on the characters' adventures in the book.

■ **Syllabication**

> *Information Literacy Standards: 1, 2, 9*
> *NCTE/IRA Standards for English Language Arts: 4, 11, 12*

Teach students how to identify syllables in words. Using the characters' names, model how to find the syllables by writing *Horace, Morris*, and *Dolores* on the board or a transparency. Use slash marks to identify the chunks or segments of each word (Hor/ace, Mor/ris, De/lor/es). Next, model how to clap out the syllables as a whole group. Ask the class to "say it, clap it, snap it, and stomp it." This strategy will reinforce students' ability to work with syllables. Make a list of other words from the book to work on syllabication. Read the book aloud once without stopping. Reread the book stopping at each word on the list chosen for syllabication practice. Pause at the identified word and use the "say it, clap it, snap it, stomp it" method with students. As a supplement, have students examine the syllabication of these words in a dictionary or use the Merriam Webster online dictionary for Kids at <www.wordcentral.com/>.

■ **Phoneme/Sound Manipulation**

> *Information Literacy Standards: 1, 2, 9*
> *NCTE/IRA Standards for English Language Arts: 4, 11, 12*

Use the following words from the story for phoneme/sound manipulation activities: Horace, sail, climb, friend, cheese, friendship, downhearted. Say the following, "Say

Summary

Three friends, Horace, Morris, and Dolores, do everything together. These adventurous mice find themselves in a bind when Horace and Morris join "Mega-Mice," a boys club that does not allow girls. Dolores finds her own club to join, but misses Horace and Morris. Frustrated, Dolores creates a brand new club where every mouse can belong regardless of gender.

Horace." Students repeat. "Now take away the /h/ and replace with /m/. What do you have?" (Morris). Then say the following, "Say friendship." Students repeat. "Now take away the ship and what do you have? (friend). Then say the following, "Say clubhouse." Students repeat. "Now take away the club and what do you have?" (house). "Now take away the /h/ and replace with /m/, what do you have?" (mouse). "Now take away the /m/ and replace with /bl/ what do you have? (blouse). Continue this process with additional words. For work with letter identification, use letter names instead of sounds.

■ Friendship Bracelet

Make a class list of qualities found in a good friend. Write these characteristics on chart paper or the board and refer to it during the reading as the qualities of friendship are discovered between the mice. Using string and beads, allow students to make a friendship bracelet for someone special by simply supplying string for the bracelet and beads for stringing. Encourage students to give the bracelet to a special friend or loved one.

Exploration: During Reading

While reading the text, stop and point out the dialogue bubbles used by the characters while speaking.

Reading Between the Lines: Post Reading

■ Checking for Comprehension: Discussion Questions

Information Literacy Standards: 4, 5, 7, 9
NCTE/IRA Standards for English Language Arts: 1, 3, 4, 11, 12

1. Describe the friendship between Horace, Morris, and Dolores.
2. Describe some of the places the three friends went on their adventures. Do you think you would have enjoyed these adventures? Why/Why not?
3. What decision did Horace and Morris make that changed everything? Has a friend ever turned his back on you? Explain how this made you feel.
4. What occurred that changed the situation for the better?

■ Rhyming Game

Information Literacy Standards: 1, 2, 3, 9
NCTE/IRA Standards for English Language Arts: 4, 11, 12

The title of the book used three names that rhyme, Horace, Morris, and Dolores. Play a rhyming game with students' names in the class. Say a student's name and ask the class to come up with other names or words that rhyme. Remind students that spelling may differ in words that rhyme.

■ Dialogue Writing (grades two and up)

Information Literacy Standards: 1, 2, 6, 9
NCTE/IRA Standards for English Language Arts: 3, 4, 5, 6, 11, 12

Throughout the text, the author indicates dialogue through the use of both dialogue bubbles and quotation marks. Teach students the correct usage of quotation marks and emphasize that quotation marks are used when a character speaks and does not contain the narration. Write this example on the board: *After Max woke up from his nap he said I would like a snack.* Ask students to answer the following questions: What did Max say in this sentence? (I would like a snack)

1. How do you know this? (the word said)
2. Show students where the quotation marks are placed. ("I would like a snack.")
3. Point out that a comma is needed after "said" and a period at the end of the quotation is located inside the quotation marks (he said, "I would like a snack.")

If necessary, perform additional drills on the use of quotation marks to ensure students comprehend this skill. To culminate this lesson, distribute a piece of paper folded with six panels. Students can work with a partner to write and illustrate a cartoon using quotation marks. After students have mastered the use of quotation marks, move on to dialogue bubbles. They can use the same cartoon, but this time the words go in the bubbles. Show students examples from the book and cartoons from the newspaper.

▪ Sequencing

Information Literacy Standards: 1, 2, 3, 6, 9
NCTE/IRA Standards for English Language Arts: 1, 3, 4, 11, 12

Explain to students that a story has a beginning, middle, and end. They must be able to distinguish what happened and in the order it happened. Using the sentences shown on page 30 in Figure 2.2, Sequencing, ask students to cut apart and paste in order on a piece of construction paper. Students can do this individually or with a partner. If working with a partner, students should read each sentence aloud to practice fluency while reinforcing the ability to sequence.

Beyond the Text: Lesson Extensions

▪ Author Study

Information Literacy Standards: 1, 2, 3, 4, 5, 6, 8, 9
NCTE/IRA Standards for English Language Arts: 1, 3, 4, 7, 8, 11, 12

Visit the web site <http://books.scholastic.com/teachers/authorsandbooks/authorstudies/authorhome.jsp?authorID=1832&displayName=Author%20Interview%20>. Have students read the transcript and the accompanying interview about James Howe. Students may find it interesting to hear how and when the author writes, how he develops characters, and other information related to his craft. As a whole class, develop a list of questions about related topics for which students are still curious. Use the Internet to search for answers to the class questions.

To extend the lesson, have students interview one another about how they write and develop characters.

Sequencing

Directions: Cut into sentence strips. Paste sentence strips on a piece of construction paper in the order in which the events occured in the story.

Dolores wondered as she watched her friends step through the door of the Mega-Mice clubhouse.
Dolores has a decision to make. She didn't really want to do anything without Horace and Morris, but she figured a girl mouse must do what a girl mouse must do.
Horace and Morris but mostly Dolores loved adventure.
And the next day they build a clubhouse of their own.
Horace and Morris but mostly Dolores never said, "This is something we shouldn't do." They said, "This is something we've got to do!"
"I'm Chloris," said the girl. "Now where can we go to have some *real* fun around here?"
I'll bet Horace and Morris couldn't do that, she thought. But she wasn't smiling as she stepped through the door of the Cheese Puffs clubhouse.
The five friends spent the rest of the day exploring. Chloris and Boris and Horace and Morris, but mostly Dolores.
Outside, Dolores introduced herself. "I'm Dolores."

Sequencing. Figure 2.2

■ Letter Writing

Information Literacy Standards: 1, 2, 3, 6, 9
NCTE/IRA Standards for English Language Arts: 4, 5, 6, 11, 12

Have students imagine they are either Horace or Morris and write a letter to Dolores explaining why it was important for them to join a "boys only" club.

■ Create a Classroom Clubhouse

Students can create a classroom club. As a whole group activity, draft the requirements to belong to the classroom club. Students can create a name, logo, and even a secret handshake. This approach can create a sense of community in the classroom.

■ Syllable Breaks

Learning to recognize syllables helps students spell and understand words. Compile a list of words from the story and distribute it to students. Using the word processor, have students type the word. Ask students to say each word and listen to the syllable breaks. Have students retype the word showing the syllables. Do this by inserting a forward slash between syllables (De/lor/es). Students print their work, get a dictionary (or use an online dictionary), and look up each word. They can compare their syllable breaks with those in the dictionary.

The Brand New Kid

Copyright date: 2000
Author: Katie Couric
Recommended age range: four to nine

Discovery and Discussion: Setting the Stage for Reading

■ **Words for Review:** squealed, shrill, taught, tease, forlorn, accent, pastry, strudel, poodle

Summary

Lazlo S. Gazky came to this country from Hungary. His first days at school are a nightmare. Because he looks different from the other students at Brookhaven School, students begin to tease him. Two classmates, Ellie and Carrie, befriend Lazlo and realize that being the "new kid" can be difficult.

■ **Friendship Outline**

Information Literacy Standards: 1, 2, 3, 4, 5, 9
NCTE/IRA Standards for English Language Arts: 4, 5, 6, 11, 12

Divide the class into manageable groups and give each group a large piece of butcher paper and markers. Ask one student to lie on the butcher paper as another student traces an outline of that student. Each group brainstorms qualities that make a friend. Write the word on the body part from which it comes. For example, a friendship quality might be "says nice things." This phrase would be written where the mouth would be on the outline. Challenge students to be creative in their lists. When all groups have completed the task, students share the qualities listed in their outlines. While students are sharing their qualities, compile a whole group outline for display on a bulletin board. While reading the story, revisit the outline to determine if the characters in the book have those same qualities.

■ **Graphing**

Create a graph showing the number of students who have attended your school since kindergarten, first grade, and so forth. Use *Microsoft Excel*™ to publish the graph. Have a discussion of what it means to be "the new kid" in class. Has anyone ever been the new kid in class? If so, have that student describe the feelings, fears, anxiety, or excitement involved.

■ **Prediction**

Look at the cover of the book. Ask students, "Do you think this student is having a good day or a bad day?" Have students support their answers using the illustration.

Exploration: During Reading

■ **Rhyme Find**

Information Literacy Standards: 1, 2, 3, 4, 5, 6, 9
NCTE/IRA Standards for English Language Arts: 1, 3, 4, 6, 11, 12

Read the book through once and inform students that many words rhyme in the book. Reread the text, this time stopping at the end of each page. Ask students to listen carefully and indicate the rhyming words. Ask students to think of other words that rhyme and make a list on the board.

Reading Between the Lines: Post Reading

■ Shower Curtain Rhyme Toss

Information Literacy Standards: 1, 2, 3, 4, 5, 6, 9
NCTE/IRA Standards for English Language Arts: 1, 3, 4, 6, 11, 12

Use a plastic shower curtain and divide it into a "Tic Tac Toe" game board using a permanent marker. Choose words or pictures to use for this activity. Print the words or draw the pictures large enough to take up a portion of the game board. Place the shower curtain game board on the floor. Students stand around the shower curtain and take turns throwing a beanbag onto the shower curtain. The student must say the word or picture on which the beanbag lands, and then say a word that rhymes with or begins with the same sound as the word or picture. Adapt according to students' abilities.

■ Bookmark Book Report

Information Literacy Standards: 1, 3, 4, 5, 9
NCTE/IRA Standards for English Language Arts: 3, 4, 5, 6, 11, 12

After reading *The Brand New Kid*, have students create a bookmark. Cut white paper (8"x11") into five equal parts. Give each student a strip of paper. On one side have students write the book's title and author and a summary of the story. On the flip side, they can illustrate a scene from their favorite part of the story and make a list of vocabulary words from the story. Laminate each student's bookmark. Use a hole punch to make a hole at the top of each bookmark. Finish with string or ribbon. (Note: this activity can also be done using the computer).

■ Writing Prompts

Information Literacy Standards: 3, 5, 9
NCTE/IRA Standards for English Language Arts: 4, 5, 6, 11, 12

Use the following prompts to encourage writing:
- ■ I am unique because…
- ■ Three qualities of a friend are…
- ■ I am a good friend when I…

Beyond the Text: Lesson Extensions

■ Welcome Letter/*PowerPoint*™ Presentation

Information Literacy Standards: 1, 2, 3, 4, 5, 6, 8, 9
NCTE/IRA Standards for English Language Arts: 4, 5, 6, 8, 11, 12

Have students imagine that several new students will be arriving in class next week. Assign students to write letters to these "newcomers" describing the students in the class, class procedures, and other pertinent information a new student needs to know about the classroom routines. For younger students, write a whole group letter to share. For older students, assign each small group to compose their own letter. Instruct students to prepare a *PowerPoint* presentation highlighting the classroom routines and procedures described in their letter.

■ **Synonyms/Antonyms**

Information Literacy Standards: 1, 3, 4, 5, 9
NCTE/IRA Standards for English Language Arts: 4, 5, 6, 11, 12

Review the definitions of synonyms and antonyms with students. Remind students that a synonym is a word that means the same, and an antonym is a word that means the opposite. Use the Synonyms/Antonyms guided practice in Figure 2.3 on page 36. A Synonyms/Antonyms Answer Key is provided below in Figure 2.4.

Word	Synonym	Antonym
forlorn	sad	cheerful
delight	joy	sorrow
shrill	high-pitched	low
swell	good	bad
mess	clutter	clean
far	distant	close
dark	dim	bright

Sentence construction: Answers will vary.

Synonyms/Antonyms Answer Key. Figure 2.4

After students work on the skill of identifying synonyms and antonyms, introduce the thesaurus, as the "synonym/antonym dictionary." Give students a word from the story and require them to find a synonym and antonym using the thesaurus.

■ **Word Wall Wizard**

Information Literacy Standards: 1, 3, 4, 5, 9
NCTE/IRA Standards for English Language Arts: 4, 5, 6, 11, 12

Using the review words or other vocabulary terms, write each word on a piece of tag board and hang on the wall. Label these words "Word Wall." Make a spinner to use for Word Wall Wizard. Use a piece of heavy tag board or cardboard and divide it into eight equal parts. Write the following categories on the spinner:

1. Say any word. Say a word that means the same (synonym).
2. Find a word that ends in a vowel.
3. Read any word. Tell how many syllables it has.
4. Choose any word. Say a word that rhymes with it.
5. Find a word that ends with a consonant.

Synonyms/Antonyms

Directions: Write a synomym and antonym in the pace provided.
Follow the example given.

Word	Synonym	Antonym
Example: *forlorn*	*sad*	*cheerful*
delight		
shrill		
swell		
mess		
far		
dark		

Sentence construction:

Part I: Write a sentence using each word in the synonym column.

_____

_____

Part II: Write a sentence using each word in the antonym column.

_____

_____

Synonyms/Antonyms. Figure 2.3

6. Spell any word. Ask a classmate to name the word and find it on the wall.

7. Say any word. Ask a classmate to use it in a sentence.

8. Choose any word. Say a word that means the opposite (antonym).

9. Give each child (you can use groups or partners) a chance to spin the spinner and do what it says. For younger students simply spin the spinner and have the students perform the task all together. Use sight words or one-syllable words for younger students.

Additional Book Selections, Professional Resources, and Web Connections on Peer Acceptance

Barnwell, Ysaye. *No Mirrors in My Nana's House*. Harcourt Children's Books, 1998. Ages five-eight.
   A young girl discovers the beauty in herself by looking into her Nana's eyes. A multicultural selection.

Blume, Judy. *Blubber*. Atheneum, 2002. Ages nine-twelve.
   Jill goes along with the rest of the fifth-grade class in tormenting a classmate and then finds out what it is like when she, too, becomes a target. Award winning author.

Brown, Don. *Odd Boy Out: Young Albert Einstein*. Houghton Mifflin, 2004. Ages five-eight.
   An introductory book about the work and early life of the great twentieth-century physicist who frustrated his teachers and had few friends because of his weight and big, misshaped head. BCCB Blue Ribbon Nonfiction Book Award. ALA Notable Children's Book. Younger Readers Award.

Bunting, Eve. *Your Move*. Harcourt, 1998. Ages five-eight.
   When ten-year-old James' gang initiation endangers his six-year-old brother Isaac, they find the courage to say, "Thanks, but no thanks." A multicultural selection.

Carle, Eric. *The Grouchy Ladybug*. HarperTrophy, 1996. Ages five-eight.
   A grouchy ladybug, looking for a fight, challenges everyone she meets regardless of their size or strength. Award winning author.

Chen, Chih-Yuan. *Guji Guji*. Kane/Miller Publishers, 2004. Ages five-eight.
   This story deals with issues about identity, loyalty, and what it really means to be a family. Guji Guji makes some big decisions about who he is, what he is, and what it all means. A multicultural selection. ALA Notable Children's Book. Younger Readers Award.

Clements, Andrew. *Jake Drake Bully Buster*. Simon and Schuster, 2001. Ages seven-ten.
   Fourth-grader Jake Drake relates how he comes to terms with SuperBully Link Baxter, especially after they are assigned to be partners on a class project.

Clements, Andrew. *Janitor's Boy*. Simon and Schuster, 2001. Ages five-eight.
   Fifth grader Jack finds himself the target of ridicule at school when it becomes known that his father is one of the janitors, and he turns his anger onto his father.

Clugston, Chynna. *Queen Bee.* Scholastic, 2005. Ages eight-twelve.
Haley is smart, funny, nice, and determined to be super-popular in her new middle school.

Cook, Julia. *A Bad Case of Tattle Tongue.* CTC Publishing, 2006. Ages five-eight.
Josh the Tattler does not have any friends. He tattles on his classmates, on his brother, and even on his dog. He tattles so much that he wakes up one night to find that his tongue is yellow, unusually long, and covered in bright purple spots.

Day, Shirley. *Luna and the Big Blur: A Story for Children Who Wear Glasses.* Magination Press, 2000. Ages five-eight.
A young girl who hates her glasses learns to appreciate them after spending a day without them.

DeRubertis, Robert. *Wally Walrus.* Kane, 1998. Ages five-eight.
Bad experiences with a bully make Wally the Walrus balk at going to school before he learns to call upon his natural abilities to prove himself.

English, Karen. *Hot Day on Abbott Avenue.* Houghton Mifflin, 2004. Ages five-eight.
After having a fight, two friends spend the day ignoring each other, until the lure of a game of jump rope helps them to forget about being mad. ALA Notable Children's Book.

Gorman, Carol. *Dork in Disguise.* HarperCollins, 2000. Ages eight-twelve.
Starting middle school in a new town, brainy Jerry Flack changes his image from "dork" to "cool kid," only to discover that he'd rather be himself.

Gorman, Carol. *Dork on the Run.* HarperCollins, 2003. Ages eight-twelve.
Having reluctantly agreed to run for sixth-grade president, Jerry, who has been trying to change his image as a dork, finds his opponent playing dirty tricks on him.

Greene, Stephanie. *Owen Foote, Second Grade Strongman.* Clarion, 1996. Ages five-eight.
Owen, a second grader who is being teased for his small size, discovers that his friend, Joseph, is just as concerned about being overweight, and they share their fear of being humiliated by the school nurse.

Hall, Bruce. *Henry and the Kite Dragon.* Philomel, 2004. Ages five-eight.
Two rival groups of children representing two different cultures come face to face, and when they do, they find they share much more than just the same sky. A multicultural selection. Irma S. and James H. Black Honor Award for Excellence in Children's Literature.

Hicks, Betty. *Out of Order.* Roaring Brook, 2005. Ages nine-twelve.
Sophomore Colt Trammel loves baseball and his girlfriend Grace, but he hates the rest of high school and maintains a tough facade to hide his feelings of inferiority. BCCB Blue Ribbon Fiction Book Award.

Jenkins, Emily. *Five Creatures.* Farrar, Straus, & Giroux, 2001. Ages five-eight.
In words and pictures, a girl describes the three humans and two cats that live in her house, and details some of the traits that they share. Boston Globe-Horn Book Honor Book.

Krishnaswami, Uma. *The Happiest Tree: A Yoga Story.* Lee and Low, 2005. Ages five-eight.

> An Asian Indian-American girl lacks the confidence she needs to appear in a school play. A multicultural selection.

Lovell, Patricia. *Stand Tall Molly Lou Melon.* Penguin, 2001. Ages five-eight.

> Even when the class bully at her new school makes fun of her, Molly remembers what her grandmother told her and she feels good about herself.

Ludwig, Trudy. *My Secret Bully.* Tricycle Press, 2005. Ages five-eight.

> When Monica's friend Katie begins to call her names and humiliate her in front of other kids at school, she feels betrayed and isolated. With help from her mother, Monica reclaims her confidence from a bully disguised as her friend.

Morgan, Nicola. *Chicken Friend.* Candlewick, 2005. Ages ten-twelve.

> When her eccentric parents suddenly move their family to a new home, an insecure girl discovers the downside of changing herself to fit in.

Moss, Peggy. *Say Something.* Tilbury House, 2004. Ages five-eight.

> A child who never says anything when other children are being teased or bullied finds herself in their position one day when jokes are made at her expense and no one speaks up.

Munson, Derek. *Enemy Pie.* Chronicle Books, 2000. Ages five-eight.

> Hoping that the enemy pie that his father makes will help him get rid of his enemy, a little boy finds that instead it helps make a new friend. Peace Education Fund Children's Book Award, Children's Choice Book Nominee, Reading Rainbow Selection.

Myers, Christopher. *Wings.* Scholastic, 2000. Ages five-eight.

> Ikarus Jackson, the new boy in school, is outcast because he has wings, but his resilient spirit inspires one girl to speak up for him. A multicultural selection.

Paterson, Katherine. *Jacob Have I Loved.* HarperTrophy, 1991. Ages nine-twelve.

> Sarah Louise, who lives with her family on a Chesapeake Bay island, grows up feeling less important than her twin sister, until she finally begins to find her own identity. Newbery Award.

Pomerantz, Charlotte. *You're Not My Friend Anymore.* Dial, 1998. Ages five-eight.

> Molly and Ben are best friends and share everything until they have a fight. A multicultural selection. Award winning author. Parents' Choice Silver Honor.

Raschka, Chris, et al. *Yo! Yes?* Weston Woods, 2000. Ages five-seven.

> Two lonely characters, one black and one white, meet on the street and become friends. Caldecott Honor Book.

Reider, Katja. *Snail Started It.* North South, 1998. Ages five-eight.

> By calling Pig fat, Snail starts a chain of insults among the other animals that eventually catches up with him and convinces him that each animal is right in liking himself just the way he is.

Rodman, Mary and E. B. Lewis. *My Best Friend*. Viking, 2005. Ages five-nine.
It is summertime at the neighborhood pool. Lily has her best friend, Tamika, chosen. Tamika already has a best friend and does not care about Lily, no matter how hard Lily tries to impress Tamika. A multicultural selection. 2003 Coretta Scott King Illustrator Award.

Shannon, David. *A Bad Case of Stripes*. Blue Sky, 1998. Ages five-eight.
In order to ensure her popularity, Camilla Cream always does what is expected, until the day arrives when she no longer recognizes herself.

Shin, Sun Yung. *Cooper's Lesson*. Children's Books, 2004. Ages eight-twelve.
When Cooper, a biracial Korean-American boy, feels uncomfortable trying to speak Korean in Mr. Lee's grocery, his bad behavior eventually leads to a change in his attitude. A multicultural selection.

Silverstein, Shel. *The Giving Tree*. HarperCollins, 1986. Ages five and up.
A moving parable about the gift of giving and the capacity to love, told throughout the life of a boy who grows to manhood and a tree that selflessly gives him her bounty through the years.

Spinelli, Jerry. *Loser*. HarperCollins, 2003. Ages nine-twelve.
Even though his classmates from first grade on have considered him strange and a loser, Donald Zinkoff's optimism and exuberance and the support of his loving family do not allow him to feel that way about himself. Newbery author.

Spinelli, Jerry. *Who Put That Hair in My Toothbrush?* Little, Brown, 2000. Ages nine-twelve.
The sibling rivalry between twelve-year-old Megin and her older brother Greg intensifies after she ruins his science project and he retaliates by throwing her favorite hockey stick into the pond. Newbery author.

Spinelli, Jerry. *Wringer*. HarperCollins, 1998. Ages nine-twelve.
As Palmer comes of age, he must either accept the violence of being a wringer at his town's annual Pigeon Day or struggle to find the courage needed to confront his peers and act according to his conscience. Newbery Award.

Wells, Rosemary. *Timmy Goes to School*. Viking, 2000. Ages five-eight.
Timothy learns about being accepted and making friends during the first week of his first year at school. Award winning author.

Wells, Rosemary. *Yoko*. Hyperion, 1998. Ages five-eight.
When Yoko brings sushi to school for lunch, her classmates make fun of what she eats until one of them tries it for himself. Award winning author.

Yangsook, Choi. *Name Jar*. Bantam Doubleday, 2003. Ages five-eight.
After Unhei moves from Korea to the United States, her new classmates help her decide what her name should be. A multicultural selection.

Professional Resources

Borba, Michele. *Nobody Likes Me, Everybody Hates Me: The Top 25 Friendship Problems & How to Solve Them.* Jossey-Bass, 2005.

> This text teaches children the 25 most essential friendship-building skills that kids need. It is essentially a guide for adults to help kids survive the social jungle without joining the wrong element.

Elman, Natalie M. and Eileen Kennedy-Moore. *The Unwritten Rules of Friendship: Simple Strategies to Help Your Child Make Friends.* Little, Brown, 2003.

> This resource offers practical strategies to sharpen any child's social skills by pinpointing the child's particular social strengths and difficulties.

Frankel, Fred. *Good Friends Are Hard to Find: Help Your Child Find, Make & Keep Friends.* Perspective, 1996.

> Based on the UCLA Children's Social Skills Program, this book offers researched-based strategies for helping five- to twelve-year-olds make friends. Offers concrete help for teasing, bullying, and meanness, both for the child who is picked on and for the tormentor.

Kaufman, Gershen. *Stick Up for Yourself: Every Kid's Guide to Personal Power & Positive Self-Esteem.* Free Spirit, 1999.

> This guide discusses problems facing young people such as making choices, learning about and liking yourself, and solving problems.

Romain, Trevor. *Cliques, Phonies, & Other Baloney.* Free Spirit, 1998.

> A discussion of cliques, what they are and their negative aspects is presented along with advice on helping children form healthier relationships and friendships.

Web Connections

Character Counts
<www.charactercounts.org/howto/teaching-tools.htm>

> This Web site offers free character-building materials including lessons plans, worksheets, and activities that promote reading and writing skills as well as help students develop ethical values and positive attitudes.

Kids' Health
<http://websrv01.kidshealth.org/parent/emotions/feelings/tolerance.html>

> Provided on this Web site is a wealth of lesson plans, articles, and related resources dealing with children's feelings, emotions, and behavior to assist in teaching tolerance.

Tolerance
<www.tolerance.org>

> Visit this Web site for ideas on ways to alert people of all ages to problems of hate and intolerance.

Chapter 3

Accepting Differences

Looking After Louis

Copyright date: 2004
Author: Lesley Ely
Recommended age range: five to ten

Discovery and Discussion: Setting the Stage for Reading

■ **Words for Review:** wobbled, recess, twinkled, crinkled, whooshed, expert

Summary

Because Louis has autism, his behavior and repetition of other people's words makes him stand out from the other students, but it is Louis who teaches the lesson that everyone is special.

■ **Before You Read**

Read the back cover of the book prior to reading being sure to emphasize the word *autism*. Ask students "Has anyone ever heard of the word autism?" "Do you know what autism is?" Spark a discussion of autism. Explain that one of the classic characteristic behaviors of a student with autism is repetition of words and phrases. Read page three and nine to demonstrate how Louis repeats phrases.

Look at the illustration on page ten that depicts Mrs. Kumar sitting with Louis, but does not explain who she is. Now would be an appropriate time to explain that Mrs. Kumar is Louis's aide, an adult who helps Louis with his schoolwork.

Finally, read the last page of the book that explains autism. Continue a discussion of autism. Clarify any misconceptions students may have at this time.

■ **Prereading/Prediction**

Information Literacy Standards: 1, 2, 6, 9
NCTE/IRA Standards for English Language Arts: 3, 4, 11, 12

Show students the title and illustration on the cover of the book. Write "Looking After

Louis" on the board. Ask students to predict what this title might mean. Write students' predictions on the board or butcher paper to revisit after the reading is complete.

Exploration: During Reading

■ Checking for Comprehension

Stop after each page of text and ask students to describe Louis's actions.

Reading Between the Lines: Post Reading

■ Using a Venn Diagram

> Information Literacy Standards: 2, 3, 4, 5, 6, 9
> NCTE/IRA Standards for English Language Arts: 3, 7, 11, 12

Distribute the Venn diagram shown in Figure 3.1 on page 45 to each student. Ask students to work individually or with a partner to complete the diagram. Students are to list the qualities and characteristics of "me," "Louis," and "both." Ask students to think of qualities that they have and list those in the "me" column. Next, ask students to think of the qualities of Louis that they do not have and list those in the "Louis" column. Finally, students list the qualities that they have in common with Louis and write those qualities in the "both" section of the diagram. Make a transparency and compose a class list to initiate discussion. For younger students, complete this as a whole group activity.

■ Puppet Retelling

> Information Literacy Standards: 1, 2, 5, 6
> NCTE/IRA Standards for English Language Arts: 1, 3, 4, 7, 11, 12

Copy or draw pictures of the main characters in the book. Reinforce drawings by gluing to tag board or construction paper. Glue each character to a Popsicle® stick or straw to make puppets. Make an adequate amount of puppet sets to accommodate several small groups. Distribute a set to each group and ask students to take turns retelling parts of the story using the puppets.

■ Writing Prompts

> Information Literacy Standards: 3, 5, 9
> NCTE/IRA Standards for English Language Arts: 4, 5, 6, 11, 12

Ask students to write to the following prompts in their journals:

1. I accept others by…
2. I am like Louis because…
3. I am different from Louis because…

After students have completed their writing, they can share with the class.

Venn Diagram

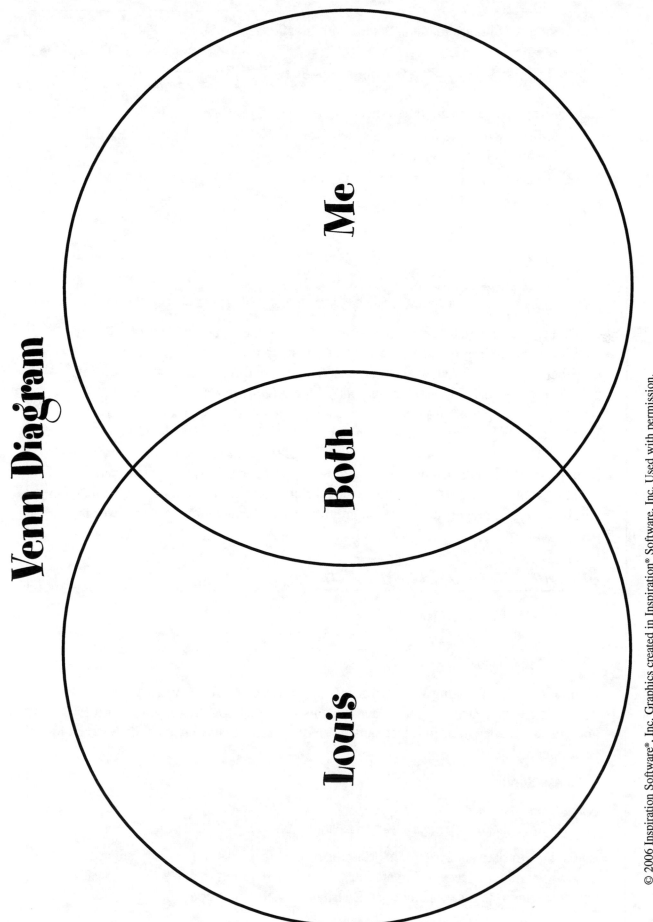

Me

Both

Louis

© 2006 Inspiration Software®, Inc. Graphics created in Inspiration® Software, Inc. Used with permission.

Venn diagram. Figure 3.1

■ Checking for Comprehension: Discussion Questions

Information Literacy Standards: 4, 5, 7, 9
NCTE/IRA Standards for English Language Arts: 1, 3, 4, 11, 12

Ask students the following questions:

1. Miss Owlie does something special for Louis. What does she do? Explain why this is so special.
2. Explain why Louis repeats what others say.
3. Describe Louis.
4. Describe Miss Owlie.

■ Point of View

Information Literacy Standards: 1, 2, 3, 5, 6, 7, 9
NCTE/IRA Standards for English Language Arts: 1, 3, 4, 5, 6, 11, 12

Explain to students that several people may describe the same incident in different ways or have varying points of view. Ask students to think about the following: 1) how their own point of view about an experience may differ from that of a sibling, parent, or classmate; 2) from whose point of view *Looking After Louis* is told; 3) how the story might be different if told from a different character's point of view. Divide students into groups. Ask them to brainstorm how the story would change from Mrs. Owlie's point of view, Louis's point of view, the boys' on the playground point of view, or the narrator's point of view. After students have brainstormed how the story might change, ask them to write a brief description of the new story that will be told. If time permits, have the groups rewrite the story in their own words in paragraph form.

Beyond the Text: Lesson Extensions

■ Creating Words from a Name

Information Literacy Standards: 3, 5, 9
NCTE/IRA Standards for English Language Arts: 11, 12

Using Figure 3.2, Creating Words from a Name, on page 48 find a word beginning with each letter in each category. Have students work individually or with a partner. For an extra challenge or for older students, require them to have two or more words in each category.

■ Recess Survey

Information Literacy Standards: 1, 2, 3, 5, 6, 7, 9
NCTE/IRA Standards for English Language Arts: 1, 3, 4, 5, 6, 7, 11, 12

Louis likes to play soccer with his classmates during recess. Inform students that they will conduct a Recess Survey. Each student is required to ask five classmates what their favorite recess activity is. Distribute the Recess Survey in Figure 3.3 on page 49. Instruct students to make an X in the appropriate column after they interview their classmates. Tailor the graph to meet students' needs according to their age, ability, or interest levels. After all surveys are completed, make a class survey graph on the board, a transparency, chart paper or create one in *Microsoft Excel*. Ask students to share their results orally. Have students enter their data on the class survey graph. After the master survey graph is completed, require students to explain the graph in writing. Emphasize phrases such as "the least" and "the most." For younger students, write a class paragraph/explanation.

■ Create a Name Logo

Distribute a piece of white drawing paper, markers, crayons, or colored pencils to students. Instruct students to print their first name on the drawing paper. Ask students to think of their favorite hobbies and interests in relation to the letters in their name. Each letter of their name will represent an activity they enjoy. For example, the letter "l" could be a hockey stick; the letter "o" could be a soccer ball. Share the name logos with the class.

Creating Words From a Name

	City	State	County	Fruit	Vegetable	Animal	Famous Person
L	Example: London						
O							
U							
I							
S							

Directions: In the space proided, write a word beginning with each letter for each category.

Creating Words from a Name. Figure 3.2

Recess Survey

	Soccer	Kickball	Jump Rope	Running	Baseball	Softball	Other
Student 1							
Student 2							
Student 3							
Student 4							
Student 5							

Directions: Place an X in the appropriate after interviewing your classmates.

Recess Survey. Figure 3.3

The Ugly Duckling

Copyright date: 2001
Author: Hans Christian Anderson
Illustrators: Maria Mantonvani and Renzo Barsotti
Recommended age range: four to nine

Summary

This is the classic fairy tale of the Ugly Duckling who grows up to be a swan and learns that appearances are not everything.

Discovery and Discussion: Setting the Stage for Reading

■ **Words for Review:**

brood, meadow, duckling, poultry, reeds, moor, teeming, shabby

■ **Prereading**

Information Literacy Standards: 3, 4, 9
NCTE/IRA Standards for English Language Arts: 4, 11, 12

Ask students the following questions prior to reading:

1. What does it feel like to be different from everybody else? Do you ever feel that way?
2. Tell about a time you didn't "fit in."
3. Have you ever been teased? If so, how did that make you feel?

■ **What Do We Already Know?**

Information Literacy Standards: 3, 4, 9
NCTE/IRA Standards for English Language Arts: 4, 11, 12

Ask students to share with the class what they might already know about ducks or ducklings. Record the information on the board, chart paper, or a transparency under the heading "What We Know." Ask students to listen carefully to the story details to discover something they didn't know about ducks or ducklings. After reading, ask the question, "What new details do you learn from the text?" and record the information. This strategy reinforces listening skills during the read aloud.

Exploration: During Reading

Take time to point out the illustrations of the duckling. Although Hans Christian Anderson is the author, each version of the book has different illustrators.

■ **Prediction of Vocabulary**

Information Literacy Standards: 3, 5, 9
NCTE/IRA Standards for English Language Arts: 11, 12

Choose developmentally appropriate vocabulary words that describe the following categories of story grammar: characters, setting, problem, and solution. Write the vocabulary words on index cards. Using a pocket chart, instruct students to predict the words that would best fit into each category. For example, Ugly Duckling would be categorized under the heading characters; barnyard would be categorized as setting. Revisit the students' predictions after reading the text.

Reading Between the Lines: Post Reading

■ Story Hand

Information Literacy Standards: 4, 5, 7, 9
NCTE/IRA Standards for English Language Arts: 1, 3, 4, 11, 12

Give each student a white piece of drawing paper. Ask students to draw an outline of their hand on the paper. Instruct students to write the following five W's on each finger:

- Thumb: Who? (Characters)
- Pointer Finger: When? Where? (Setting)
- Middle Finger: What? (Beginning)
- Ring Finger: What? (Middle)
- Pinky: What? (End)
- Palm of the Hand: Problem (Conflict) & Solution (Resolution)

Discuss story structure with students, i.e., all stories have a beginning, a middle, and a conclusion (end). Read the story again slowly providing ample wait time for students to record the story details on the correct part of the hand. Students can use the hand to retell the story to a partner or the class. In planning for this strategy, prepare ahead of time a white glove with the appropriate story grammar written on it to retell the story to the class. Model this strategy before having students do it.

■ Checking for Comprehension: Discussion Questions

Information Literacy Standards: 4, 5, 7, 9
NCTE/IRA Standards for English Language Arts: 1, 3, 4, 11, 12

Ask students the following questions for discussion:

1. Was the duckling actually ugly? Were there any characters in the story that were truly ugly? If so, what made them ugly?
2. Why didn't the duckling feel welcome in the old woman's house or the barnyard?
3. Why did the wild ducks and the swans seem to accept the duckling? Why did they invite him to join them?
4. Ugly was a swan the entire time, but he didn't know it. What would make you feel like a swan?

■ Share a Different Version

Have the librarian/library media specialist acquire several different versions of *The Ugly Duckling* to share with students. Compare the illustrations in each version. Pay special attention to how the duckling is portrayed.

- **Duckling Poem**

Information Literacy Standards: 1, 2, 3, 4, 5, 9
NCTE/IRA Standards for English Language Arts: 1, 3, 4, 5, 6, 11, 12

Instruct students to write a poem from the duckling's point of view. Hold a poetry reading in the classroom or library and invite other classes and parents to attend.

Beyond the Text: Lesson Extensions

- **Readers Theater/Create a Mask**

Information Literacy Standards: 1, 2, 3, 4, 5, 6, 7, 9
NCTE/IRA Standards for English Language Arts: 1, 3, 4, 5, 6, 8, 11, 12

Have students create a paper mask for an animal in the story. Students can paint or draw the details of the face. Create a Readers Theater script and allow students to act out the parts. Older students can write the script themselves in small groups. Students can also create a mural with barnyard scenes or a pond.

- **Barnyard Banquet**

Allow each student to be a different animal from the story. Have students make sandwich boards indicating the name of the animals they are portraying. If time permits, have students make costumes to wear. Hats with the animal's name are also an alternative. Allow students to design a "menu" for the event. Pose questions such as, "What would a cow or a chicken want to eat at a banquet? What would they do at the banquet?" Use the Internet to help students research their areas of interest.

Oliver Button Is a Sissy

Copyright date: 1990
Author: Tomie dePaola
Recommended age range: five-eight

Discovery and Discussion: Setting the Stage for Reading

■ *Words for Review:* tap dance, tap shoes, routine, accordion, master of ceremonies

■ **Exploring Feelings**

Have a student read the book's title. Ask students to define or explain the word, "sissy." Ask students to imagine that someone called them a sissy. Ask students, "How does it make you feel when someone calls you a name?" and "What should you do when this happens?"

■ **Exploring Gender Stereotyping**

Summary

Oliver Button exhibits many special talents that make him unique. Oliver likes to draw, read, and, most of all, Oliver likes to tap dance. Because he is not interested in the same activities that others boys his age are involved with such as football and baseball, the boys tease him and call him a sissy. Despite the taunting from his classmates, Oliver follows his own path being true to himself, and, ultimately, earns the respect of his classmates because of his tenacious self-respect.

Information Literacy Standards: 1, 2, 6, 9
NCTE/IRA Standards for English Language Arts: 5, 11, 12

Make a chart with three columns on the board or a transparency. Label the first column "activity;" the second, "Boys;" and the third column, "Girls." Write the following phrases from the story in column one: playing football, tap dancing, reading books, dressing up in costume clothes, playing with dolls, walking in the woods, playing a musical instrument. Ask students to decide if the activity is something that boys mostly do or something that girls mostly do. Place a checkmark in the appropriate "Boys" or "Girls" column after students respond to each activity. If time permits, ask students to identify other things that they believe are "only for boys" and "only for girls." Save the chart for discussion after reading the story. For older students, give each student a worksheet with the information and allow them to work with partners or groups before sharing as a whole group.

Exploration: During Reading

Stop reading periodically to discuss Oliver's thoughts and feelings using the illustrations as a springboard.

Reading Between the Lines: Post Reading

■ **Story Comprehension**

Information Literacy Standards: 4, 5, 7, 9
NCTE/IRA Standards for English Language Arts: 1, 3, 4, 11, 12

Select the questions/prompts that are appropriate for your students.

1. Give some examples of Oliver's activities that the other boys in his class considered "sissy" activities. Refer to the chart that was created in the Gender Stereotyping strategy. Follow with a discussion on why they associate certain activities with boys and certain activities with girls.

2. How do you think Oliver felt when students made fun of him? Do you think these boys have the right to react that way to Oliver? Why/Why not?

3. How do you feel about what happened to Oliver in the story?

4. Why do you think Mama and Papa enrolled Oliver in dance school? Do you think that was a good idea? Why/Why not?

5. What was Oliver's dance teacher's name?

6. Who won the talent show contest?

7. How does Oliver feel after the contest?

8. Recall the message on the wall at the end of the story indicating that Oliver is now a star. What does the message mean?

9. What was so special about the way Oliver solved the problem?

10. Ask students to predict what may have happened if Oliver did not participate in the talent show.

11. Ask students to brainstorm words to describe Oliver's character traits.

■ Class Brick Wall

Information Literacy Standards: 1, 2, 3, 4, 5, 6, 8, 9
NCTE/IRA Standards for English Language Arts: 1, 3, 4, 5, 6, 7, 8, 11, 12

Review the story and point out the name-calling and the bullying that Oliver experienced. Explain that Oliver had to have a great deal of courage to help him persevere and continue tap dancing and doing the other things he enjoyed even when students were making fun of him. Using library books on quotations or a Web site on quotations (<www.bartleby.com/quotations/>), have students look up courage quotations. Create a class graffiti wall using a large piece of butcher paper (72" x 90"). Draw lines on the paper to simulate a brick-like look. Have students take turns writing their quotation in one of the bricks. Additional bricks can be created where students can draw illustrations. The "wall" can be displayed in the library or outside the classroom.

■ Story Sharing Retelling

Information Literacy Standards: 1, 2, 5, 6, 7, 9
NCTE/IRA Standards for English Language Arts: 1, 3, 4, 7, 11, 12

To improve and assess comprehension, have students find partners and, in their own words, tell their favorite part of the story to their partner.

■ Sissy Acrostic Super Words

Information Literacy Standards: 1, 3, 4, 5, 9
NCTE/IRA Standards for English Language Arts: 4, 5, 6, 11, 12

Write the word *sissy* on the board or a transparency. Build an acrostic poem by asking students to brainstorm complimentary words based on the word sissy. Have students write a sentence using each of these complimentary words. For older students have students write an essay containing each of the complimentary words.

■ Acrostic Poetry with Kindness

Information Literacy Standards: 1, 3, 4, 5, 9
NCTE/IRA Standards for English Language Arts: 4, 5, 6, 11, 12

Review the fact that Oliver's classmates exhibited bullying behaviors and were unkind to Oliver. Have students brainstorm ways of being kind to one another. Have students create a Kindness Web using Figure 3.4 on page 56. Allow each student to share ideas and suggestions on being kind from each category. Follow the discussion by composing an acrostic kindness poem. Have students write the word *kindness* vertically on the left side of the paper. On each line, write a related word that begins with each letter that demonstrates an act of kindness.

■ E-Kindness Card

Information Literacy Standards: 1, 3, 4, 7, 8, 9
NCTE/IRA Standards for English Language Arts: 4, 5, 6, 8, 11, 12

Using the following Web site, <www.actsofkindness.org/inspiration/ecards.asp> have students create an e-card to send to one of their classmates.

■ Writing to the Author

Information Literacy Standards: 1, 2, 3, 4, 5, 6, 7, 8, 9
NCTE/IRA Standards for English Language Arts: 4, 5, 6, 7, 8, 11, 12

Explain to students that authors enjoy getting letters from their readers. Explain that the author of this book, Tomie dePaola, is a renowned children's author. Students can visit his Web site at <www.eduplace.com/kids/hmr/mtai/depaola.html>.

Have students visit the library to find the author's contact information and write a letter to the author. Suggest students include these items in the body of the letter: 1) age and grade; 2) favorite part of the book; 3) favorite characters and scenes from the story that they enjoyed; and 4) describe what they learned from reading the story and how it has impacted their behavior. The author's contact information can be found at <www.tomie.com/about_tomie/contact.html>.

Beyond the Text: Lesson Extensions

■ Talent Show

Have students make up a song, choreograph a dance, or demonstrate a unique talent, such as performing a magic trick as the Great Mystro did in the story. Give a live performance in class. The talent show could be presented to parents or the community.

Kindness Web

Classmates

Example: Saying "please" and "thank you."

Animals

Family

Kindness

Environment

Teachers

Neighbors

Directions: List the way you can show acts of kindness under each category.

Kindness Web. Figure 3.4

■ Let's Dance

Information Literacy Standards: 1, 2, 6, 7, 8, 9
NCTE/IRA Standards for English Language Arts: 3, 4, 5, 6, 7, 8, 11, 12

Because Oliver performed a tap dance at the talent show, have students research the history of tap dance on the Internet and write a paragraph about what they learned in their journal.

■ Book Review

Information Literacy Standards: 1, 2, 3, 5, 8
NCTE/IRA Standards for English Language Arts: 4, 5, 6, 8, 11, 12

Have students write a book review and post it to the library's Web site.

■ Kindness Buttons

Information Literacy Standards: 3, 4, 5
NCTE/IRA Standards for English Language Arts: 4, 5, 6, 11, 12

Have students create a button with a kindness slogan. Slogans can be as simple as, "Be Kind." Buttons may be displayed in the library, classroom, or hallway. Students may also exchange buttons to wear.

Additional Book Selections, Professional Resources, and Web Connections on Accepting Differences

Arvella, Wendy. *Pray for a Rainbow*. Island Heritage, 2001. Ages five-eight.
Kimo's new friend Emily is diagnosed with cancer. Through his artwork he brings joy and comfort to her. A multicultural selection.

Bang, Molly. *Tiger's Fall*. Random House, 2003. Ages nine-twelve.
After eleven-year-old Lupe is partially paralyzed in an accident in her Mexican village, other handicapped people help her realize that her life can still have purpose. A multicultural selection.

Bertrand, Diane Gonzales. *My Pal, Victor/My Amigo*. Raven Tree Press, 2004. Ages five-eight.
Two Latino boys experience camaraderie, despite one's disability. A multicultural selection.

Clements, Andrew. *Brave Norman: A True Story*. Simon & Schuster Children's Publishing, 2002. Ages five-eight.
Norman, a blind Labrador retriever, saves a girl from drowning in the ocean.

Deans, Sis. *Rainy*. Henry Holt, 2005. Ages seven-twelve.
Ten-year-old Rainy Tucker, who has Attention Deficit Hyperactivity Disorder, leaves her family for the first time to go to sleep-away camp in rural Maine. Award winning author.

Debear, Kirsten. *Be Quiet, Marina*. Star Bright, 2001. Ages five-eight.
A noisy little girl with cerebral palsy and a quiet little girl with Down's Syndrome learn to play together and eventually become best friends.

Dorros, Arthur. *Julio's Magic*. HarperCollins. 2005. Ages five-eight.
A young artist discovers the power of friendship when he helps his mentor, who is going blind, win a prestigious woodcarving contest. A multicultural selection.

Fox, Mem. *Whoever You Are*. Voyager, 2001. Ages five-eight.
Despite the differences between people around the world, there are similarities that join us together, such as pain, joy, and love. A multicultural selection. Reading Rainbow Feature.

Gantos, Jack. *Joey Pigza Loses Control*. HarperTrophy, 2002. Ages nine-twelve.
Joey, who takes medication for ADD to keep him from getting too wired, goes to spend the summer with the hard-drinking father he has never known and tries to help the baseball team he coaches win the championship. Newbery Honor Book.

Goldin, Barbara Diamond. *Cakes and Miracles: A Purim Tale*. Puffin, 1993. Ages five-eight.
Blinded by a childhood illness, young blind Hershel finds that he has talents to help his mother during Purim. A multicultural selection.

Hallinan, P. K. *A Rainbow of Friends*. Ideals, 2002. Ages five-eight.
Demonstrates universal acceptance among all cultures, races, and handicaps among people. A multicultural selection.

Herrera, Juan Felipe. *Featherless/Desplumado*. Children's Book Press, 2004. Ages five-eight.
At his new school or on the soccer field, everyone wants to know why Tomasito is in a wheelchair. His father gives Tomasito a new pet to make him smile, but this bird is a little bit different. A multicultural selection.

Katz, Karen. *The Color of Us*. Owlet, 2002. Ages five-eight.
Seven-year-old Lena and her mother observe the variations in the color of their friends' skin, viewed in terms of foods and things found in nature. A multicultural selection.

Lears, Laurie. *Ian's Walk: A Story About Autism*. Whitman, 2003. Ages five-eight.
A young girl realizes how much she cares for her autistic brother Ian when he gets lost at the park.

Lester, Julius. *Shining*. Silver Whistle, 2003. Ages five-eight.
A young girl who has not uttered a sound since birth is shunned by the people in her village, until they realize how special she is. A multicultural selection.

Mason, Ashley. *Everybody Is Somebody Special*. Publish America, 2004. Ages five-eight.
Two chipmunks struggle for their own identity, and it is intended to encourage young children to be their own individual person. The chipmunks and

their furry playmates realize that everyone is different and that everyone offers something special and unique to the world.

Mitchell, Lori. *Different Just Like Me*. Charlesbridge, 2001. Ages five-eight.
While preparing for a visit to her grandmother, a young girl notices that, like the flowers in Grammie's garden, people who are different from one another also share similarities and it's okay to like them all the same. The Parent Council Award. Early Childhood News Directors' Choice Award.

Parr, Thomas. *It's Okay to Be Different*. Megan Tingley, 2001. Ages five-eight.
Illustrations and brief text describe all kinds of differences that are "okay," such as "It's okay to be a different color," "It's okay to need some help," "It's okay to be adopted," and "It's okay to have a different nose."

Riggs, Stephanie. *Never Sell Yourself Short*. Whitman, 2001. Ages eight-twelve.
Fourteen-year-old Josh was born with achondroplasia, the most common form of dwarfism. In this photo-essay, Josh talks about his life, describing the challenges he faces along with his plans for the future.

Robbs, Diane B. *The Alphabet War*. Whitman, 2004. Ages five-eight.
This book discusses the intellectual and emotional struggles that children with dyslexia experience.

Rodriguez, Bobbie. *Sarah's Sleepover*. Penguin Putnam, 2000. Ages five-eight.
Sarah is blind and she has invited her five cousins for a sleepover. When a fuse blows out and leaves the girls in the dark, Sarah comes to the rescue. A multicultural selection.

Ryan, Pam Munoz. *Becoming Naomi Leon*. Scholastic, 2004. Ages nine-twelve.
When Naomi's absent mother resurfaces to claim her, Naomi runs away to Mexico with her great-grandmother and younger brother who is physically challenged in search of her father. Americas Award Honor Book.

Shriver, Maria. *What's Wrong with Timmy?* Little, Brown, 2001. Ages five-eight.
Making friends with a mentally retarded boy helps Kate learn that the two of them have a lot in common.

Thomas, Pat. *Don't Call Me Special: A First Look at Disabilities*. Barron's, 2002. Ages five-eight.
This text explores questions and concerns about physical disabilities and encourages children to confront social and emotional issues that sometimes present problems.

Thompson, Mary. *Andy and His Yellow Frisbee*. Woodbine, 1996. Ages five-eight.
The new girl at school tries to befriend Andy, an autistic boy who spends every recess by himself, spinning a yellow Frisbee under the watchful eye of his older sister.

Weeks, Sarah. *So B. It*. Laura Geringer, 2004. Ages nine-twelve.
After spending her life with her mentally retarded mother whose vocabulary is made up of 24 words, and agoraphobic neighbor, 12-year-old Heidi sets

out from Reno, Nevada to New York to discover the truth about who she is. Booklist Editor's Choice. Books for Youth Award.

Willis, Jeanne. *Susan Laughs.* Holt, 2000. Ages five-eight.
Rhyming couplets describe a wide range of common emotions and activities experienced by a little girl who uses a wheelchair.

Wojtowicz, Jennifer. *The Boy Who Grew Flowers.* Barefoot Books, 2005. Ages five-eight.
Rink takes a new student, Angelina, who has a physical disability, under his wing.

Woloson, Eliza. *My Friend Isabelle.* Woodbine House, 2003. Ages five-eight.
Isabelle and Charlie are friends. They both like to draw, dance, read, and play at the park. They both like to eat Cheerios. They both cry if their feelings are hurt. And like most friends, they are also different from each other. Isabelle has Down's Syndrome. Charlie does not.

Wong, Janet S. *Apple Pie 4th of July.* Harcourt, 2002. Ages five-eight.
A Chinese-American child fears the food her parents prepare won't be eaten. A multicultural selection. Asian Pacific American Award for Literature.

Professional Resources

Jaeger, Paul T. and Cynthia Ann Bowman. *Understanding Disability: Inclusion, Access, Diversity, and Civil Rights.* Praeger Greenwood, 2005.
A holistic understanding of the lives of individuals with disabilities from representations in the media to issues of civil rights is presented.

Kluth, Paula. *You're Going to Love This Kid: Teaching Students with Autism in the Inclusive Classroom.* Brookes, 2003.
Guide to understanding students with autism and including them fully in the classroom. Includes specific ideas for enhancing literacy; planning challenging, multidimensional lessons; supporting student behavior; connecting, communicating, and collaborating; fostering friendships; and adapting the physical environment.

Lavoie, Richard. *It's So Much Work to Be Your Friend: Helping the Child with Learning Disabilities Find Social Success.* Touchstone, 2006.
This text offers practical strategies to help children with learning disabilities ages six through seventeen navigate the treacherous social waters of their school, home, and community. It also examines the special social issues surrounding a wide variety of learning disabilities, including ADD and other attention disorders, anxiety, paralinguistic, visual-spatial disorders, and executive functioning.

Web Connections

Inclusion
<http://inclusion.ngfl.gov.uk>
> This Web site is an online catalog of resources to support individual learning needs and inclusion; part of the British government's National Grid for Learning.

Resources for Special Education
<http://curry.edschool.virginia.edu/go/specialed>
> This site from the Curry School of Education at the University of Virginia contains a wealth of information about special education, including the history of the field, types of disabilities, and strategies for working with students with special needs.

Responsive Classroom
<www.responsiveclassroom.org>
> This online magazine focusing on strategies for fostering safe, challenging, and joyful classrooms and schools, kindergarten through eighth grade.

Chapter 4

Death of a Family Member

Blackberries in the Dark

Copyright date: 1985
Author: Marvis Jukes
Recommended age range: seven to eleven

Discovery and Discussion: Setting the Stage for Reading

- **Words for Review:** died, fly fishing, galoshes, blackberries

- **Packing Your Bags**

> Information Literacy Standards: 3, 5, 9
> NCTE/IRA Standards for English Language Arts: 4, 8, 11, 12

Since Austin is going to spend ten days on his grandparent's ranch, ask students to think about items they might bring with them if they were going on a similar trip. Because some students will not be familiar with ranch life, use the Internet to investigate. The following Web site is a good starting point for students: <www.pbs.org/wnet/ranchhouse/visit.html>. As students conduct research, ask them to compare and contrast their clothes and other necessities to that of ranch life. Using a bulletin board or wall space, draw a large suitcase on brown tag board and ask students to fill the suitcase with words describing what they might bring with them on the trip to the ranch.

Summary

Jukes, a Newbery Honor Author, tells the story of Austin, who is heartbroken when his grandfather passes away and wonders what he will do for ten days at his grandmother's house. Austin was looking forward to learning to fly fish and other traditions that he and his grandfather shared. Together, Austin and his grandmother learn how to keep memories of Grandpa alive while they begin some new traditions of their own. The story tells the tale of grief and love.

■ **Family Traditions**

Information Literacy Standards: 4, 9
NCTE/IRA Standards for English Language Arts: 4, 5, 6, 11, 12

Ask students to interview a member of the family or a family relative and document what family traditions exist in their own families. Students then write a first-person narrative about a family tradition of their own to share with the class and families.

Exploration: During Reading

■ **Character Map**

Information Literacy Standards: 2, 3, 5
NCTE/IRA Standards for English Language Arts: 1, 2, 3, 12

While reading the story, add elements to the Character Map in Figure 4.1 on page 65 as the characteristics of Austin unfold.

Reading Between the Lines: Post Reading

■ **Postcard Connection**

Information Literacy Standards: 2, 3, 5
NCTE/IRA Standards for English Language Arts: 1, 2, 3, 4, 5, 6, 12

After reading the story, ask students to take the voice of the main character, Austin, to write postcards to friends or family at home. Writing in the voice of the main character will enhance their understanding of Austin's feelings about being at the ranch without his grandfather. Teach students how to address a postcard properly. A postcard template is provided in Figure 4.2 on page 66.

■ **Bedtime Stories**

Information Literacy Standards: 5, 9
NCTE/IRA Standards for English Language Arts: 1, 2, 3, 4, 8, 10, 11, 12

Austin recalls the bedtime stories that his grandfather used to tell him when he was younger. Ask students to recall their favorite bedtime story or the librarian/school library media specialist can help students find a suitable story. Audiotape the students as they read these stories and pass them along to the kindergarten teacher to use in centers. This activity will build fluency as students practice their reading.

■ **Rewriting the Plot**

Information Literacy Standards: 2, 3, 4, 5
NCTE/IRA Standards for English Language Arts: 1, 2, 4, 5, 6, 11, 12

As Austin and his grandmother create new traditions, the story takes a new turn. Ask students to rewrite the traditions in the story. How would the story change? Would they change the story's ending?

Character Map

Directions: Answer each question in a complete sentence.

 What does the character look like?

 Who are the character's family and friends?

 What does the character do or say?

 What is the character's challenge?

 How does the character deal with the challenge?

 How will you deal with the challenge?

Character's name

Character Map. Figure.4.1

Postcard Template

Dear: _____

_____
_____
_____
_____   _____
_____   _____
_____   _____
_____
_____

Front

Back

Postcard Template. Figure 4.2

Beyond the Text: Lesson Extensions

■ Blackberry Jam/Writing Connection

Information Literacy Standards: 2, 3, 9
NCTE/IRA Standards for English Language Arts: 4, 5, 6, 11, 12

Austin and his grandfather ate blackberries in the dark. Have students work together in groups to create blackberry jam. The recipe is given below. Of course, you must eat it in the dark! If making jam is not possible, bring in blackberry jam for students to taste. Students write an explanatory essay on how they made their jam or how it would be made based on the recipe provided. Emphasis on transition words is essential to this type of writing.

Blackberry Jam Recipe
(makes two 12-ounce jars)

Ingredients:

- two quarts fresh blackberries
- 1/2 cup water
- 3/4 cup orange juice
- three Tbsp lemon juice
- six cups sugar
- one Tbsp grated orange peel
- candy thermometer

Steps:

1. Cook berries with water until heated. Strain to remove most of the seeds. Add the orange and lemon juices, sugar and orange peel to mixture.
2. Cook rapidly to the jellying point, until it reaches 220 degrees F on a candy thermometer.
3. Pour boiling hot mixture into hot jars: adjust the lids. Cook for 10 minutes in a boiling-water bath. Start the counting time when the water returns to a boil.
4. Remove the jars from the water and cool on a rack.
5. Eat and enjoy (in the dark)

Everett Anderson's Goodbye

Copyright date: 1983
Author: Lucille Clifton
Recommended age range: five to eight
Awards: Coretta Scott King Award, NCTE Teacher's Choice, Reading Rainbow Feature

Discovery and Discussion: Setting the Stage for Reading

■ *Words for Review:* denial, bargaining, depression, anger, acceptance

■ **Concept Map**

Information Literacy Standards: 4, 5, 9
NCTE/IRA Standards for English Language Arts: 11, 12

Students complete the Vocabulary Concept Map in Figure 4.3 on page 69 both before and after reading the text. Prior to reading, ask students to discuss the concept of "grief" by completing the concept map provided. This process affords the opportunity to tap into students' background knowledge. For younger students guide them through this lesson by making a class concept map on the board or a transparency.

■ **Picture Walk**

Information Literacy Standards: 4, 5
NCTE/IRA Standards for English Language Arts: 1, 3, 11, 12

Review illustrations on pp. 1, 3, 9, 11-12, 15-16, 19-20 of the story text.

- ■ Ask students to predict from the illustrations what the story will be about. Record the predictions on the board, chart paper, or a transparency.
- ■ Ask students to pay special attention to what Everett is doing, as well as his facial expressions. Does he look happy or sad? How do you know? What makes you think that? Have you ever felt the way Everett might feel in the book?

■ **RIVET Vocabulary Lesson (grades two and up)**

Information Literacy Standards: 2, 4, 5, 9
NCTE/IRA Standards for English Language Arts: 11, 12

This vocabulary activity, developed by Patricia Cunningham (1995), is similar to a "Wheel of Fortune" game where the librarian/school library media specialist or teacher utters each letter in a word slowly, until students can guess the word. Next, have students write a prediction of the story based on the vocabulary words *denial, anger, bargaining, depression, acceptance,* and *grief.* Use the RIVET reproducible provided in Figure 4.4 on page 70. The Rivet answer key is provided in Figure 4.5 on page 71.

Summary

When Everett Anderson's father dies, he progresses through the phases of mourning. Although recommended for ages five to eight, this story is universal in approach because it captures all human conflicting emotions. Dominated by pencil sketches, this story brings to the forefront the stages of grief (denial, anger, bargaining, depression, and acceptance) and human emotion felt in a time of mourning. This book is a multicultural selection.

Vocabulary Concept Map

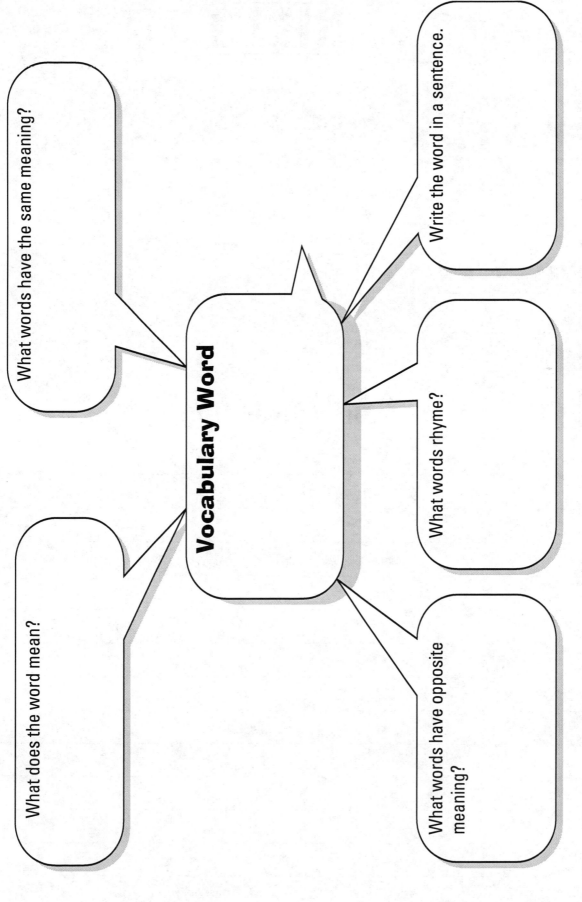

What words have the same meaning?

What does the word mean?

Vocabulary Word

Write the word in a sentence.

What words rhyme?

What words have opposite meaning?

Directions: Complete each section of the Vocabulary Concept Map using the vocabulary word provided.

Vocabulary Concept Map. Figure 4.3

RIVET

1. __ __ __ __ __ __

2. __ __ __ __

3. __ __ __ __ __ __ __

4. __ __ __ __ __ __

5. __ __ __ __ __ __

6. __ __ __ __ __

Story Prediction

_____

_____

_____

_____

_____

_____

_____

_____

_____

_____

RIVET. Figure 4.4

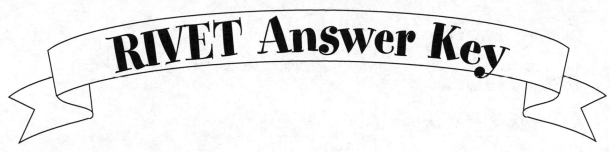

RIVET Answer Key

1. <u>D e n i a l</u>
2. <u>A n g e r</u>
3. <u>B a r g a i n i n g</u>
4. <u>D e p r e s s i o n</u>
5. <u>A c c e p t a n c e</u>
6. <u>G r i e f</u>

Story Prediction

Answers will vary

_____

_____

_____

_____

_____

_____

_____

_____

_____

_____

_____

RIVET Answer Key. Figure 4.5

Exploration: During Reading

Stop and confirm or revise predictions throughout the read-aloud checking for comprehension during reading.

Reading Between the Lines: Post Reading

■ Concept Map

Information Literacy Standards: 4, 5, 9
NCTE/IRA Standards for English Language Arts: 11, 12

Revisit the original concept map students made in the Discovery and Discussion: Setting the Stage for Reading section on page 68. Revise the definition of the word "grief." Ask students how their definition changed? Stayed the same? What could be added to the definition? What could you exclude? Have students look up the word in the dictionary. Discuss the dictionary definition and compare it with students' definitions.

■ Schema Activation (If applicable to student population)

Information Literacy Standards: 2, 3, 4, 5, 9
NCTE/IRA Standards for English Language Arts: 4, 11, 12

Determine if there is a student who has experienced a loss who is willing to share the experience with the class. Allow those students an opportunity to discuss how they felt. Is their experience similar to or different from Everett Anderson's experience? Can they relate to him in any way? Who helped Everett in his time of grief? Who helped you in your time of grief? If students have not had this particular experience, allow them to make some predictions as to how they may feel. Have you witnessed others going through something similar? What were your impressions?

Beyond the Text: Lesson Extensions

■ Vocabulary Lesson: Word Family Word Sort

Information Literacy Standards: 3, 5, 9
NCTE/IRA Standards for English Language Arts: 11, 12

Using the words in the text that end in the suffix "*ing*," students can categorize the words working with a partner or in a small-group setting. Theoretically, this closed word sort determines how the students will categorize the words according to word structure. The purpose of word sorting is to assist students in focusing on phonological features of words and their patterns. Using the Word Family Word Sort in Figure 4.6 on page 73, students cut the words into two parts: the base word and the suffix "*ing*."

Word Family Word Sort

Directions: Cut the words into two parts: 1) the base word and) the suffix "ing." Example: The word waving would be cut into two parts. The first part would be "wav" and the second part would be "ing." "wav" would be the base word; "ing" would be the suffix.

walking	waving
caring	laughing
staring	turning
talking	standing

Word Family Word Sort. Figure 4.6

The Fall of Freddy the Leaf: A Story of Life for All Ages

Copyright date: 1982
Author: Leo Buscaglia
Recommended age range: seven and up

Discovery and Discussion: Setting the Stage for Reading

- **Words for Review:** nature, spring, autumn (fall), summer, winter

- **Listening Lesson**

> Information Literacy Standards: 3, 5, 9
> NCTE/IRA Standards for English Language Arts: 1, 4, 9, 11, 12

Listen to the song, "Circle of Life," from *The Lion King* soundtrack. Ask students to interpret the lyrics and why they think the songwriter chose those words. Lyrics are available at <www.lionking.org/lyrics/OMPS/CircleOfLife.html>

- **Discussion Starter**

> Information Literacy Standards: 5, 9
> NCTE/IRA Standards for English Language Arts: 7, 8, 11, 12

Ask students to close their eyes and imagine they are a leaf. Using the five senses, brainstorm a list of what the children see, hear, smell, taste, and touch. Write this list on chart paper for reference while reading the text.

Discuss the seasons with students. What are the jobs of the leaves during each season? Use props and ask four students to dress in the seasonal props. For example, give a student a light jacket and an umbrella to portray spring. Ask students what season is being conveyed by each volunteer.

Collect leaves from outside. Each student creates a leaf rubbing of his own leaf and names it. Ask students what job their leaf will perform and during what season. If your geographical area limits this activity, use the Internet or library books to research and investigate different types of leaves found in other areas of the United States.

Exploration: During Reading

- **Checking for Comprehension: Discussion Questions**

> Information Literacy Standards: 4, 5, 7, 9
> NCTE/IRA Standards for English Language Arts: 1, 3, 4, 11, 12

1. How does Freddy know that summer is coming to an end?
2. How do the leaves feel as the wind begins to tug at their stems?

Summary

Freddy, a maple leaf, is born in the spring and soon learns about himself, his fellow leaves, and his surroundings. He learns that he is a part of nature and has a very important role in this process. Freddy learns about the differences between himself and the other leaves. Using the metaphor of the seasons, Freddy learns that like life, leaves must change and eventually "let go."

3. Why do you think Freddie does not get scared when spring changes into summer, or summer into autumn?
4. How do you feel when Daniel lets go?
5. When you look at the pictures in this book, what tells us that the seasons are changing?
6. What happens to the leaves after they fall to the ground?
7. What is the meaning/importance of the last two words of the story?

Reading Between the Lines: Post Reading

■ Autumn Haiku (grades two and up)

Information Literacy Standards: 4, 5, 6
NCTE/IRA Standards for English Language Arts: 4, 5, 6, 9, 11, 12

Students write a haiku about autumn. Instruct children that a haiku has three lines consisting of five syllables (line one), seven syllables (line two) and five syllables (line three). Review syllables by counting or clapping out the syllables of a word. This process will reinforce the essential reading skills of phonemic awareness and phonics instruction. Ask students to read their haikus aloud. The haikus can be displayed in the library or the classroom. For younger children, this activity can be completed as a whole group writing a class haiku or story.

Beyond the Text: Lesson Extensions

■ Construct a Life Size Tree/Sentence Writing (If space permits)

Information Literacy Standards: 5, 6, 9
NCTE/IRA Standards for English Language Arts: 4, 5, 6, 11, 12

Trace a three- or four-foot tree on brown butcher paper and cut it out. Use as a bulletin board or hallway display.

Materials:
- brown butcher paper
- green construction paper
- orange construction paper
- brown construction paper
- scissors
- tape
- leaf template (See Figure 4.7 on page 76)

Give each student a leaf template and one piece each of green, orange, and brown construction paper. Students trace three leaves from each color of paper. After the leaves are traced and cut out, students write a sentence on each leaf. On the green leaf students write a sentence about how the leaf feels to be alive. On the orange leaf students write a sentence about how the leaf feels about dying. On the brown leaf students write a sentence about how the leaf feels about being dead.

Leaf Template

Leaf Template. Figure 4.7

Story Frame

Directions: Complete the story Frame with
the information learned in the story.

The story, _____ is about
(Title of book)

_____

_____

_____

_____

_____

_____

The main character's name is _____.

In the story many events take place.

The first event is _____

_____

_____

The second event is _____

_____

_____

The third event is _____

_____

_____

The last event is _____

_____

_____

At the end of the story, _____

_____

_____

Story Frame. Figure 4.8

Make a life-sized tree out of the brown butcher paper. Ask students to read the sentence they wrote on each leaf and then hang the leaves in the appropriate place either on the tree (green leaves), falling from the tree (orange leaves), or on the ground near the tree (brown leaves). This can be used as a bulletin board or a display in the library.

For students who are unfamiliar with the change of seasons, students can research the characteristics of seasons. The following Web sites are useful to help students learn about the four seasons of the year: <www.windows.ucar.edu/tour/link=/the_universe/uts/seasons1.html&edu=ele>,<www.scienceu.com/observatory/articles/seasons/seasons.html>, and <www.learninghaven.com/science/articles/seasons.htm>.

■ Story Frame

Information Literacy Standards: 6, 7
NCTE/IRA Standards for English Language Arts: 1, 3, 4, 6, 11, 12

One way to improve and assess comprehension is through the use of a Story Frame shown in Figure 4.8 on page 78. Students complete the story frame after reading to display their understanding of the text and its sequential order. Additionally, the story frame reinforces the elements of literature that are vital to comprehension of fiction.

Additional Book Selections, Professional Resources, and Web Connections on Death of a Family Member

Aliki. *The Two of Them*. HarperTrophy, 1987. Ages five-eight.
A little girl and her grandfather share many happy times together until his passing where she hurt "inside and out," but will never forget him. A Reading Rainbow selection.

Barrons, T.A. *Where Is Grandpa?* Philomel, 2000. Ages five-eight.
A young boy grieves for the death of his grandfather. The family shares memories of Grandpa's adventurous life. The father answers his son's questions about where Grandpa is now.

Boyden, Linda. *Blue Roses*. Lee & Low, 2002. Ages five-eight.
Rosalie, a Native American girl, grieves the death of her grandfather. A multicultural selection.

Bunting, Eve. *Happy Funeral*. Harper Collins Children's Books, 1982. Ages five-seven.
A little Chinese-American girl pays tribute to her grandfather as she assists in the preparations for his funeral. A multicultural selection.

Bunting, Eve. *So Far From the Sea*. Clarion Books, 1998. Ages six-twelve.
Nine-year-old Laura Iwaskak and her Japanese-American family visit her grandfather's grave where Laura leaves a special memento. Issues are presented concerning the grandfather's past. Caldecott Award winning author. A multicultural selection.

Burrowes, Adjoa J. *Grandma's Purple Flowers*. Lee & Low, 2000. Ages five-eight.
A young African-American girl narrates this text about the passing of her grandmother. A multicultural selection.

Carrick, Carol. *Upside-Down Cake*. Clarion, 1999. Ages seven-ten.
Together, an unnamed nine-year-old boy and his father, who is dying of cancer, celebrate the father's last birthday.

Cooke, Trish. *The Granddad Tree*. Walker, 2001. Ages five-eight.
The author uses a tree metaphor to depict the death of Leigh and Vin's grandfather. A multicultural selection.

Creech, Sharon. *Walk Two Moons*. HarperTrophy, 1996. Ages nine and up.
Salamanca Tree Hiddle faces the truth about the loss of her mother. Newbery Award.

DePaola, Tomie. *Nana Upstairs & Nana Downstairs*. Putnam, 1998. Ages five-eight.
When the "upstairs" grandmother dies, the "downstairs" grandmother comforts him. Caldecott Award winning author.

Golds, Cassandra. *Clair de Lune*. Alfred A. Knopf, 2006. Ages seven-ten.
The story of a young girl named Claire who has not spoken since the death of her mother, a great ballet dancer, 12 years earlier.

Grimes, Nikki. *What Is Goodbye?* Hyperion, 2004. Ages eight-twelve.
Brother and sister, Jerilyn and Jesse, describe their complicated, private thoughts through poems as they grieve for their brother, Jaron. Pennsylvania School Librarians Best of the Best Children's Books Choice Award.

Hanson, Regina. *A Season for Mangoes*. Clarion, 2005. Ages five-nine.
A Jamaican girl, Sareen, describes her feelings and says her own personal goodbyes at a wake to honor her grandmother, Nana. Detailed explanation of the country's history, food, and folklore about death are given throughout the text. A multicultural book selection.

Jackson, Aarinae R. *Can You Hear Me Smiling?* Child Welfare League of America, Inc., 2004. Ages six-nine.
This story recounts with honesty, tenderness, and courage an older sister's illness, passing, and the range of emotions she experienced during this difficult time. A multicultural selection.

Kadohata, Cynthia. *Kira-Kira*. Atheneum, 2004. Ages nine and up.
Katie's older sister, Lynn, whom she idolizes, dies of lymphoma. This Japanese-American family tries to cope with their loss. Newbery Award. Pennsylvania School Librarians Best of the Best Children's Books Choice Award. A multicultural selection.

Koss, Amy Goldman. *Stolen Words*. American Girl, 2001. Ages eight-twelve.
Robyn Gittlema, whose great grandparents survived the Holocaust, comes to terms with the death of her Aunt Beth by rewriting her aunt's diary, a gift that was stolen from her luggage as she vacationed in Vienna. Many references are made to the Holocaust and the girl's Austrian-Jewish heritage. A multicultural selection.

Lanton, Sandy. *Daddy's Chair*. Lanton Haas Press, 2001. Ages five-eight.
Michael's father has died of cancer. He attempts to protect his Daddy's special

chair. Specific details on Shiva, Jewish mourning customs and traditions, are discussed. Sydney Taylor Award Winner. A multicultural selection.

Leiner, Katherine. *Mama Does the Mambo.* Hyperion, 2001. Ages five-eight.
A Cuban child, Sophia, narrates this heartbreaking story about the death of her Papa. A multicultural selection.

Lundgren, Gunilla. *Malcolm's Village.* Firefly, 1985. Ages seven-eleven.
Set in a village of Mount Kilimanjaro, seven-year-old Malcolm mourns the death of "Grandma." A multicultural selection.

Napoli, Donna Jo. *Flamingo Dreams.* Greenwillow, 2002. Ages five-eight.
Grieving over her father's death from cancer, a young girl celebrates their last year together by making a book that includes mementos and a story. A multicultural selection.

O'Dell, Scott. *Island of the Blue Dolphins.* Yearling, 1987. Ages nine-twelve.
After the death of her brother, a young Native American girl is left alone on an island off the coast of California for eighteen years. Newbery Medal.

Rubright, Lynn. *Mama's Window.* Lee & Low, 2005. Ages eight-twelve.
Eleven-year-old James Earle is faced with living with his uncle after his mother dies.

Rylant, Cynthia. *Missing May.* Scholastic, 2005. Ages seven-twelve.
Summer experiences the death of her Aunt May. Summer becomes close to her Uncle Ob as they both struggle to come to terms with Aunt May's death. Cletus, a neighbor boy, comes along to help provide an answer. Newbery Award.

Schweibert, Pat. *Tear Soup.* Grief Watch, 2005. Ages seven-ten.
A story of how "Grandy" makes a batch of tear soup to console her loss.

Strete, Craig. *When Grandfather Journeys into Winter.* Greenwillow, 1979. Ages seven-twelve.
Little Thunder comes to terms with the death of his grandfather, Tayhua. A multicultural selection.

Stroud, Bettye. *The Patchwork Path: A Quilt Map to Freedom.* Candlewick, 2005. Ages six-nine.
After Hannah's Mama dies and her sister is sold from the plantation, Hannah and her father decide to make a break for freedom. Based on a true account. A multicultural selection.

Professional Resources

Dougy Center for Grieving Children. *35 Ways to Help a Grieving Child.* Dougy Center, 1999.
This guidebook provides practical suggestions on how to support a grieving child. It discusses what behaviors and reactions to expect from children at different ages and ways to create safe outlets for children to express their thoughts and feelings.

Heegaard, Marge. *When Someone Very Special Dies: Children Can Learn to Cope with Grief.* Woodland, 1988. Ages nine-twelve.

> A practical format for allowing children to understand the concept of death and develop coping skills for life is offered.

Katz, Robert A. *Elaine's Circle.* Marlowe & Company, 2005. Ages nine and up.

> An intimate story of a dedicated teacher, a supportive community, and a group of children who refuse to let the prospect of death disrupt their classmate's schooling.

Silverman, Janis. *Help Me Say Goodbye: Activities for Helping Kids Cope When a Special Person Dies.* Fairview Press, 1999. Ages five-eight.

> Written by a family therapist, this book helps grieving children identify their feelings and learn to accept and deal with them.

Web Connections

Dr. Spock
<www.drspock.com/topic/0,1504,116+cbx_families,00.html>.

> Dr. Spock offers developmentally appropriate information on talking to children about death to help them cope with the loss.

Human Loss Links
<http://griefhealing.com/humanlosslinks.htm>.

> Extensive list of links in categories such as death of an infant, child, grandchild, parent, and sibling as well as general bereavement resources and information are provided on this Web site.

Chapter 5

Death of a Friend

Badger's Parting Gifts

Copyright date: 1984
Author: Susan Varley
Recommended age range: seven to 10

Discovery and Discussion: Setting the Stage for Reading

- **Words for Review:** death, dependable, reliable, gifts

- **Special Gifts**

  Information Literacy Standards: 3, 4, 5, 9
  NCTE/IRA Standards for English Language Arts: 11, 12

Summary

After Badger's death, his forest friends find numerous ways to cope with their grief. By sharing their memories of Badger and his many gifts, the forest friends find hope to move forward in their own lives. This story is accompanied by illustrations that bring each character to life.

In the story Badger teaches many of his friends how to do something unique or gives them a special gift. Ask students to discuss special gifts they have received or special talents that have been passed down from parents or friends. How can these talents be considered "a special gift?" Can these "special gifts" be passed on to others? How can this be?

Exploration: During Reading

- **Checking for Comprehension: Discussion Questions**

  Information Literacy Standards: 4, 5, 7, 9
  NCTE/IRA Standards for English Language Arts: 1, 3, 4, 11, 12

Questions to ask during reading:

1. Badger described the end of this life as going down a "long tunnel." What might this mean? How did Badger know that his time was limited on earth?

2. What are Badger's gifts in the story? Ask students to explain their special gifts.

3. Chart what each animal received as a "gift" and why it was viewed as such. Use the Gift Chart shown in Figure 5.1 on page 85 for discussion. Make a copy for each student or use chart paper or a transparency to display the chart. Students can complete the chart individually or as a whole group.

Reading Between the Lines: Post Reading

■ Feelings

Information Literacy Standards: 2, 3, 4, 5
NCTE/IRA Standards for English Language Arts: 1, 3, 4, 11, 12

Discuss the different feelings the characters in the story experience by creating webs for each of the characters including Badger. Ask students to identify with one or more of the characters and explain why they can identify with the character. Have students relate those personal connections to the text to improve comprehension.

■ Tea Party Strategy (grades one and up)

Information Literacy Standards: 2, 3, 4, 5
NCTE/IRA Standards for English Language Arts: 1, 3, 4, 11, 12

This activity adapted from Gail Tompkins (1998) encourages students to read or reread pre-selected excerpts from the story. Type the pre-selected excerpts from the story. Be sure to document the excerpts appropriately giving credit to the author. Mount the excerpts on tag board, laminate, and distribute to students. Students then move around the room, reading their excerpts to each other and talking about the passage they have read. Give students 10-15 minutes to move throughout the room reading the excerpts. Students return to their desks to share what they learned. This practice of reading the excerpts and discussing the story will improve students' fluency and comprehension skills.

Note: Have a tea party to celebrate the conclusion of the story. Serve tea or another suitable beverage and make gingerbread like Badger. Below is a delicious gingerbread recipe you may want to try at home.

Gingerbread Recipe
Ingredients:
- 2/3 cup shortening
- 3/4 cup of molasses
- one egg
- three cups flour
- 1/2 tsp baking powder
- 1/2 cup brown sugar

Gift Chart

Directions: Complete each column with the information you learned from the book. Next to each of Badger' friends' names, write the gift that they gave Badger and the effect it had on them. The first one is completed for you. Write your answers in complete sentences.

Badgers friends	The parting gifts	How the gifts make a difference
Example: *Mole*	*Badger taught Mole how to cut a paper chain of moles.*	*Cutting a paper chain of moles made Mole self-confident. He was proud of his accomplishment.*
Frog		
Fox		
Mrs. Rabbit		

Gift Card. Figure 5.1

- 1 tsp cinnamon
- 1/4 tsp ground cloves
- two tsp ground ginger
- Salt (a pinch)

Steps:

1. In a bowl add together the cream and the shortening, brown sugar, cinnamon, cloves, ginger, and salt. Add the egg and mix together, then add the molasses and mix once more.
2. Mix together the flour, baking powder, and baking soda in a separate bowl. Sift then add to the creamed mixture from step one. Stir ingredients until blended well and chill in refrigerator for one hour.
3. Preheat oven to 375 degrees. Roll dough one quarter at a time to 1/8" thickness on a floured board. Cut the dough with cookie cutter and then transfer to a cookie sheet.
4. Bake for eight to ten minutes.
5. Once cooled, you can decorate as you please.
6. Enjoy.

Beyond the Text: Lesson Extensions

■ I Remember Poem (grades one and up)

Information Literacy Standards: 3, 4, 5, 9
NCTE/IRA Standards for English Language Arts: 4, 5, 6, 11, 12

Have students write a poem about a special person or animal in their lives (either living or deceased). Each line of the poem begins with the words "I remember…" Indicate to students that the poem does not have to rhyme. Give students specific vocabulary words, if desired, and indicate that students should use those words to create their poem. Conduct a poetry reading where students can share their writing. Compile the students' poems into a class book and place it in the library or feature the poems on the library's Web site. Adapt for younger students by creating a "we remember" poem as a whole class. Each student must contribute one sentence orally as the librarian/school library media specialist/teacher writes the poem on the board, chart paper, or a transparency. Read and reread the poem as a whole class to reinforce sight word vocabulary and fluency. Circle unfamiliar words and create a word wall using the words from the class poem.

■ Letter Writing (grades two and up)

Information Literacy Standards: 3, 4, 5
NCTE/IRA Standards for English Language Arts: 4, 5, 6, 11, 12

In the story Badger writes a letter to his friend before he dies. Use this opportunity to teach students how to write a friendly letter of their own. Using the word processor, require students to write a rough draft, revise, and edit before creating a final draft of their letter.

I Had a Friend Named Peter: Talking to Children About the Death of a Friend

Copyright date: 1987
Author: Janice Cohn
Recommended age range: five to nine

Discovery and Discussion: Setting the Stage for Reading

- **Words for Review:** confused, die, morgue, buried

- **Preparation**

Before reading this story to students, read the introduction written by the author. The introduction provides guidelines for both educators and parents to follow as they help children deal with this sensitive topic.

Summary

After a car hits Peter, Betsy's parents have the task of telling her about the tragedy. They explain that there was nothing the doctors could do to help him survive and that children do not normally die at such a young age. They invite Betsy to attend the funeral with them. This story will give support to young children who are experiencing the death of a playmate.

- **Think, Pair, Share**

Information Literacy Standards: 4, 5
NCTE/IRA Standards for English Language Arts: 4, 11, 12

Think, Pair, Share is an instructional strategy created by Lyman (1981) to develop students' critical thinking skills. The following explains how to use the Think, Pair, Share strategy:

1. **Think.** Using the questions listed below, ask students to take a few moments just to silently think individually and brainstorm answers to the questions.

2. **Pair.** Using partners, students pair up to talk about the answer each student developed. Have students compare their mental or written notes and identify their best and most convincing answers.

3. **Share.** After students talk in pairs for a few moments, call for pairs to share their thinking with the whole class by using a round-robin method. Record these responses on the board, chart paper, or a transparency.

Before reading, use the Think, Pair, Share strategy, discuss the following:

1. What games do you play with your friends? What are other activities you share with friends? Why are these activities so important to you?

2. What is an accident? Give examples. What can happen after an accident?

Exploration: During Reading

- **Checking for Comprehension: Discussion Questions**

Information Literacy Standards: 4, 5, 7, 9
NCTE/IRA Standards for English Language Arts: 1, 3, 4, 11, 12

While reading the text, pay special attention to the discussion Betsy's parents have with her about what happens when a person dies. Ask students:

1. What happens after you die? (body goes to morgue, buried in ground, funeral, and cemetery)
2. What did Betsy do to cope with her grief? (talked about her feelings, drew a picture, and shared her feelings with others)

Reading Between the Lines: Post Reading

■ Open Mind Portraits

> *Information Literacy Standards: 2, 3, 4, 5*
> *NCTE/IRA Standards for English Language Arts: 1, 4, 11, 12*

Adapted from a strategy developed by Gail Tompkins (2003), Open Mind Portraits can help students think more deeply about a character in a book or, in this case, a classmate. There are two steps to this activity: 1) the face of the character, drawn by the student, and, 2) the mind of the character, drawn on a second page by the student. For younger students, you may consider making a template of a head to copy and distribute to each student.
Steps:

1. Draw a portrait of the character. It can be a portrait of one of the characters from the story or a portrait of the classmate/friend/family who has recently died. Students draw and color a portrait of the head and neck of the person/character they are depicting. For younger students, make a template for each character and allow the students to fill in the facial features to the best of their ability. This activity will help students realize the person/character's important traits.
2. Cut out the portrait and tape it or staple it to the top of another piece of drawing paper in order to design the mind page.
3. Students lift the portrait and draw another outline of the portrait. In this portrait they will write the person/character's thoughts or characteristics.
4. Share with classmates. Students discuss why they decided to use the words they chose.

Beyond the Text: Lesson Extensions

■ All About Books (grades one and up)

> *Information Literacy Standards: 4, 5, 9*
> *NCTE/IRA Standards for English Language Arts: 4, 5, 6, 9, 11, 12*

When dealing with a loss of a student in the classroom, a nice way to memorialize the student is by developing All About _____ Books (Sowers, 1985, Tompkins, 1998). (Note: insert deceased student's name in the blank). Create a four or five page booklet for each student to write either about their deceased classmate or the characters in the book (Betsy or Peter). Share these individualized stories. By rereading these stories, students can practice their fluency skills. These books, which can be easily bound with string or ribbon after punching holes, can become part of the classroom or school library collection or can be posted on the library's Web site.

Sadako and the Thousand Paper Cranes

Copyright date: 1977
Author: Eleanor Coerr
Recommended age range: eight to thirteen

Discovery and Discussion: Setting the Stage for Reading

■ *Words for Review:*

Leukemia, World War II, Atomic Bomb, Pearl Harbor, origami, memorial, Hiroshima, radiation

■ Prereading/KWL

Information Literacy Standards: 2, 3, 4, 5
NCTE/IRA Standards for English Language Arts: 4, 11, 12

Summary

This narrative is based on the real life story of a girl named Sadako and her battle with leukemia. After her survival of an atomic bomb during World War II, she battles cancer. Sadako learns of a Japanese myth that states if someone is able to fold one thousand paper cranes, they will be granted a wish. Sadako strives to do that.

Construct a KWL (What I Know, What I Want to Know, What I Learned) chart (Ogle, 1986) found in Figure 5.2 on page 90 based on students' prior knowledge of World War II. Before reading, students complete column one, "What I Know" individually. Conduct a class discussion and make a class list of what students already know about World War II on the board, chart paper, or a transparency. Students then complete column two, "What I Want to Know." Add this information to the class list. Have students revisit the chart as the story progresses and questions arise to record additional information. The information gathered can serve as a catalyst for student research in the library. The final column, "What I Learned," is completed at the end of the novel as a means of reviewing and summarizing or providing missing or misinterpreted information.

■ Good Luck Charms

Information Literacy Standards: 2, 4, 5
NCTE/IRA Standards for English Language Arts: 4, 11, 12

Sadako speaks of good luck signs throughout the text. Before the class begins to read, have students bring in their own good luck charms for a "show and tell." If students do not have a good luck charm, ask them to select an object that is special to them. Have them share the item and discuss why they believe it brings them good luck. An alternative is to have students either use clipart from the computer or use the Internet to find pictures of their selected items.

Exploration: During Reading

■ Family Tree

Information Literacy Standards: 3, 5
NCTE/IRA Standards for English Language Arts: 1, 3, 4, 11, 12

KWL Chart

Directions: Complete each section of the chart. Write in complete sentences.

K What I Know	W What I Want to Know	L What Did I Learn?

KWL Chart. Figure 5.2

While reading the text, construct a family tree of Sadako's family and friends. This ongoing character list will help students keep track of the ever-growing cast of characters. Create this tree on a bulletin board using leaves to represent each new character as they are introduced in the text.

■ **Vocabulary Development**

Information Literacy Standards: 3, 5, 9
NCTE/IRA Standards for English Language Arts: 11, 12

Students may encounter unfamiliar words in the text. Construct a word wall with unfamiliar words. A word wall can be a large sheet of butcher paper or strips of construction paper on which students and the librarian/school library media specialist or teacher writes interesting, confusing, and important words (Tompkins, 2003). Use this word wall to create a vocabulary game such as bingo. In addition to the traditional bingo game, try the following variation of vocabulary bingo to familiarize student with words:

1. Write the story words on an index card and place them in a box.
2. Draw two nine square bingo cards on the board. Write the story words randomly on each card.
3. Choose a student caller to draw a card from the box and read the word aloud.
4. Divide the remaining students in two groups.
5. Send a student from each team to the board. Have the student caller read the word. The player will make an X on the square that corresponds to the word called.
6. Continue by sending the next two players until one team gets a bingo.

Reading Between the Lines: Post Reading

■ **Myth Discussion**

Information Literacy Standards: 4, 5, 7, 9
NCTE/IRA Standards for English Language Arts: 1, 3, 4, 11, 12

In the story, Sadako believes that if a person creates a thousand paper cranes, his or her wish will come true. Discuss the concept of a myth, a term used throughout the text. Ask students if they believe in the thousand paper crane myth and to justify their answer. For further discussion have students find books on other myths in the library or visit the Encyclopedia Mythica Web site at <www.pantheon.org/>.

■ **Paper Cranes**

Information Literacy Standards: 1, 2, 3, 4, 5
NCTE/IRA Standards for English Language Arts: 4, 8, 9, 11, 12

Have students make paper cranes for display in the classroom. This exercise is valuable because it emphasizes skills in following directions. This exercise can be modified to reinforce listening skills by orally reading the directions to students. Directions on making a paper crane can be found at <www.csi.ad.jp/suzuhari-es/1000cranes/paperc/> or <www.paperfolding.com/diagrams/>.

Beyond the Text: Lesson Extensions

■ Picture Frames

Information Literacy Standards: 3, 4
NCTE/IRA Standards for English Language Arts: 11, 12

One way to remember someone who has died is to cherish a photograph of him or her. Students can construct picture frames for loved ones that may have passed. By using Popsicle® sticks students can make a memorial frame for someone they loved.

Materials:

- Craft sticks or Popsicle® sticks (a minimum of four per student)
- Glue
- Paint
- Photograph or copy of a photograph
- Magnetic stripping (available at a craft store)

1. Students paint their Popsicle® sticks the color of their choice.
2. After the sticks are dry, students glue them together to make a square or frame.
3. Insert photo or hand drawn illustration.
4. Decorate with sequences or other embellishments for a more delightful creation. Some may want to write the person's name on the frame, as a memorial to their lost loved one.
5. Cut a piece of magnetic stripping and place on back to hang on refrigerator or other area of interest.

Additional Book Selections, Professional Resources, and Web Connections on Death of a Friend

Bauer, Marion Dane. *On My Honor*. Yearling, 1987. Ages seven-ten.
> When his best friend, Tony, drowns while they are both swimming in a treacherous river that they had promised never to go near, Joel is devastated and terrified at having to tell both sets of parents the terrible consequences of their disobedience. Newbery Award.

Blackburn, Lynn B. and Joy Johnson. *Timothy Duck*. Centering Corporation, 1987. Ages five-seven.
> Timothy Duck talks about all the feelings he has after his favorite friend gets ill and dies. He discovers the importance of saying goodbye. He also discovers that even though he will miss his friend and remember him, life at the pond goes on.

Buck, Pearl. *The Big Wave*. HarperTrophy, 1986. Ages nine-twelve.
> A famous story of a Japanese boy who must face life after escaping the tidal wave destruction of his family and friends. Multicultural selection. Child Study Association's Children's Book Award. Pulitzer Prize Winning Author.

Bunting, Eve. *Blackwater.* HarperTrophy, 2000. Ages nine-twelve.
>   When a boy and girl are drowned in the Blackwater River, thirteen-year-old
>   Brodie must decide whether to confess that he may have caused the accident.
>   Golden Sower Award.

Carlstrom, Nancy White. *Blow Me a Kiss, Miss Lilly.* Harper Collins, 1990. Ages
five-seven.
>   When her best friend, Miss Lilly, passes away, Sara learns that the memory of a
>   loved one never dies.

Paterson, Katherine. *Bridge to Terabithia.* HarperTrophy, 1987. Ages eight-twelve.
>   The life of a ten-year-old boy in rural Virginia expands when he becomes friends
>   with a newcomer who subsequently meets an untimely death trying to reach their
>   hideaway, Terabithia, during a storm. Newbery Award.

Smith, Cynthia L. *Rain Is Not My Indian Name.* Harper Collins, 2001. Ages eight-twelve.
>   Tired of staying in seclusion since the death of her best friend, a Native American
>   girl takes on a photographic assignment with her local newspaper to cover events
>   at the Native American summer youth camp. A multicultural selection.

Smith, Doris B. *A Taste of Blackberries.* HarperTrophy, 1992. Ages seven-ten.
>   A young boy recounts his efforts to adjust to the accidental death of his best friend.

Taha, Karen T. *A Gift for Tia Rosa.* Skylark, 1991. Ages seven-ten.
>   This classic tale depicts the death of a child's elderly neighbor, Tia Rosa.
>   Carmela's mother teaches her daughter, Carmela, that she can pass on the love
>   she had for her friend, Tia Rosa to those left behind. Reading Rainbow Selection.

Wilson, Jacqueline. *Vicky Angel.* Delacorte, 2001. Ages eight-twelve.
>   After her lifelong best friend Vicky dies, Jade struggles with grief, guilt, and the
>   domineering personality of Vicky's ghost.

Professional Resources

Corr, Charles A. *Handbook Of Childhood Death and Bereavement.* Springer
Publishing Company, 1996.
>   Providing assistance to children coping with death and bereavement, this hand-
>   book covers infancy, toddler hood, early childhood, and middle childhood.

Fitzgerald, Helen. *The Grieving Child.* Fireside, 1992.
>   This handbook explains the death of a parent, relative, friend, and pet to a child
>   as well as offers suggestions for dealing with emotional responses and helping in
>   the child's adjustment to a new life.

Smith, Harold I. *Grieving the Death of a Friend.* Augsburg Books, 1996.
>   While guiding the reader through the natural grief process, this resource explores
>   the many aspects of death including the passing, the burying, the mourning, the
>   remembering, and the reconciling.

Web Connections

Center for Grieving Children
<www.grievingchildren.org/resources.html>.
   An extensive list of links providing quality information on grieving to help children cope is provided on this Web site.

Kidsource
<www.kidsource.com/sids/childrensgrief.html>.
   This site discusses common expressions of a child's grief and other ways to help children understand and cope with death.

Chapter 6

Death of a Pet

Dog Heaven

Copyright date: 1995
Author: Cynthia Rylant
Recommended age range: four to nine

Discovery and Discussion: Setting the Stage for Reading

- **Words for Review:** biscuits, clouds, geese

- **Predictions from Reading**

> Information Literacy Standards: 1, 2, 6, 9
> NCTE/IRA Standards for English Language Arts: 3, 4, 11

Before reading *Dog Heaven*, show students the cover of the book and ask them to predict what the story will be about. Write students' predictions on the board or chart paper. After reading, be sure to confirm, reject, or revise predictions.

- **Building Schema**

> Information Literacy Standards: 2, 3, 4, 5, 9
> NCTE/IRA Standards for English Language Arts: 4, 5, 6, 11, 12

Explain that the author, Cynthia Rylant, has an interpretation of what Dog Heaven looks like. Have students draw a picture or create a collage of their interpretation of what Dog Heaven may look like. Ask students to write one or two sentences to explain

Summary

Cynthia Rylant uses colorful acrylics to document the journey to Dog Heaven where there are endless fields in which to run and play, clear lakes full of geese, angel children playing, and biscuits shaped liked cats. Rylant makes Dog Heaven an accessible, friendly, and inviting place so that children have the sense that their dogs are happy and carefree. Rylant assures children that their dogs do visit Earth, invisibly, to make sure all is well.

their illustration/collage. Gather all illustrations/collages into a class book for display around the library or classroom. Creating a class book can be accomplished by three hole punching the pages and binding with ribbon or string. Laminate the book if desired.

Exploration: During Reading

■ Confirming Predictions

Information Literacy Standards: 1, 2, 6, 9
NCTE/IRA Standards for English Language Arts: 3, 4, 11, 12

Stop periodically and confirm or revise predictions made by students.

Reading Between the Lines: Post Reading

■ Comparison

Information Literacy Standards: 2, 3, 4, 5, 6, 9
NCTE/IRA Standards for English Language Arts: 3, 7, 11, 12

Compare students' interpretation of Dog Heaven with that of the author, Cynthia Rylant. Use the following questions as discussion starters:

1. What did you include that the author did not?
2. What did the author include that you would like to include in your illustration?

Beyond the Text: Lesson Extensions (appropriate for after school programs or home project)

■ Memorial Stepping Stones

Information Literacy Standards: 3, 4
NCTE/IRA Standards for English Language Arts: 11, 12

Making a stepping-stone to remember a favorite pet is a way to help children deal with a loss. The following is a list of materials and guidelines needed to create the stepping-stones:

Materials Needed:

- Two-inch deep molds e.g., cake pans, pizza boxes, plastic containers
- Concrete (fast setting)
- Facemasks
- Bucket
- Water
- Automotive oil or release spray
- Utensils to stir the cement
- Decorations such as seashells, pieces of tile, marbles
- Metal file

- Cooking oil
- One-inch hard cloth or wire screen
- Assorted paints

Steps:

1. Prepare the molds by spraying cooking oil inside the mold. (This process is necessary for removal from the molds).

2. Put facemasks on. Mix the concrete according to the directions on package. (Five parts concrete to one part water is typical. The concrete consistency will be somewhat like cookie dough).

3. Spoon or pour concrete into each mold. Fill the mold half full of concrete and then smooth. Place the hard cloth or wire screen into the mold. Fill remainder of mold with concrete.

4. Make sure all bubbles are gone by tapping the side of the mold.

5. Set time is 30 to 60 minutes. Once set, students can decorate it.

6. Allow stepping-stone to dry for a minimum of two days. Pop the stone out of the mold. Use metal file to smooth any rough edges.

7. If desired, paint it now. It is ready for display in the library, the classroom, or the garden!

I'll Always Love You

Copyright date: 1985
Author: Hans Wilhelm
Recommended age range: four to nine

Discovery and Discussion: Setting the Stage for Reading

■ *Words for Review:* squirrels, flower garden, mischief, scolded

■ **Veterinarian Visit**

> *Information Literacy Standards: 4, 5, 7*
> *NCTE/IRA Standards for English Language Arts: 4, 12*

Summary

The story of Elfie, a dachshund, and her master as they spend life together. When Elfie is a puppy, she is full of life, energy, and vigor, but as time passes, she becomes slower. Eventually Elfie dies. Each night Elfie's owner reminisces about the times they spent together and says, "I'll always love you."

Invite a veterinarian to speak to students. Prior to the visit, help students generate questions to ask the veterinarian about his/her job duties and dealing with a death of a pet. As an alternative to having a speaker in person, arrange for the guest speaker through a videocast or Webcast using the CU-SeeMe program available through Cornell University's CU-SeeMe Page at <www.webopedia.com/TERM/C/CU_SeeMe.html> or use Classroom Conferencing Online from the Global School Network at <www.gsn.org/gsh/cu/index.html>. Students can also post their questions to one of the following "Ask the Expert" Web sites: <www.askanexpert.com/>, <www.graphicmaps.com/askus.htm>, or <www.allexperts.com/>.

■ **Concept Ladder**

> *Information Literacy Standards: 3, 5, 9*
> *NCTE/IRA Standards for English Language Arts: 11, 12*

Introduce the terms *scolded* and *mischief* to students prior to reading. A Concept Ladder (Gillet and Temple, 1982) is an effective way to introduce new terms to students. Students write the word in the first step labeled "concept" and work their way up the ladder or continuum. Use this activity for any words in the text. A Concept Ladder is provided in Figure 6.1 on page 99.

Exploration: During Reading

■ **Dog Years**

> *Information Literacy Standards: 2, 3, 4, 5*
> *NCTE/IRA Standards for English Language Arts: 11, 12*

Before reading, show students the cover of the book. Ask them to predict what the story is going to be about. Read the text on page three and show students the illustrations on pages two and three. Use this text to teach students the difference between

Concept Ladder

Directions: Using the words provided by your teacher, complete each step in the Concept Ladder. An example is provided.

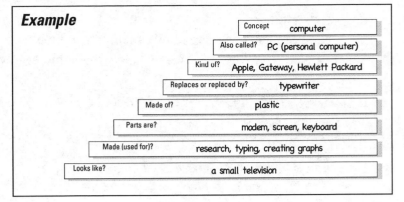

Example

Concept	computer
Also called?	PC (personal computer)
Kind of?	Apple, Gateway, Hewlett Packard
Replaces or replaced by?	typewriter
Made of?	plastic
Parts are?	modem, screen, keyboard
Made (used for)?	research, typing, creating graphs
Looks like?	a small television

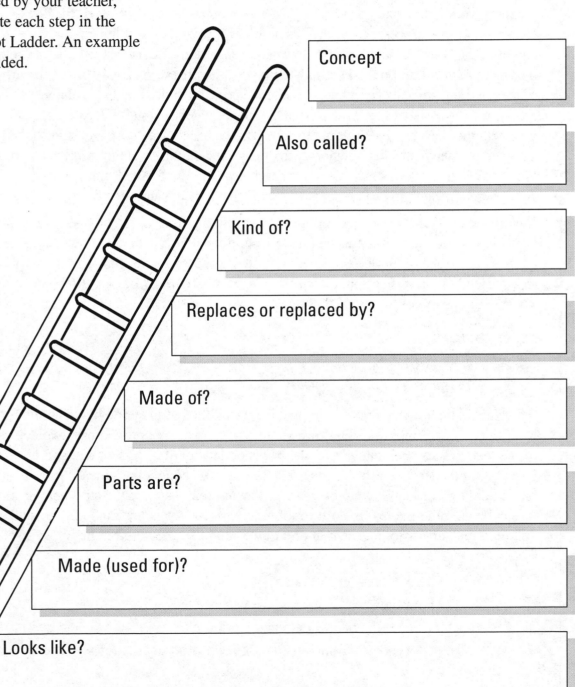

Concept

Also called?

Kind of?

Replaces or replaced by?

Made of?

Parts are?

Made (used for)?

Looks like?

Concept Ladder. Figure 6.1

dog years and human years. As a math extension, have students figure out their age in dog years. Students can ask family members to help them figure out their age in dog years as well. Use the Dog Years Chart provided in Figure 6.2 on page 101.

Reading Between the Lines: Post Reading

■ Postcards

Information Literacy Standards: 2, 3, 4, 5, 7, 9
NCTE/IRA Standards for English Language Arts: 4, 5, 6, 11, 12

Students work individually or in pairs to write the author a postcard about the book. Using the writing process, have students brainstorm what they would like to tell the author of the book. Require students to write a rough draft. Revise and edit before committing to a final draft on the Postcard Template in Figure 6.3 on page 102. On the front of the postcard, students learn how to address a postcard and write their opinions about the story or what they have learned from the story. Students can also decorate the postcard with their favorite scene from the book. On the back of the postcard, students write a paragraph with their interpretation of the story. Student may want to visit the author's Web site at <http://books.scholastic.com/teachers/authorsandbooks/authorstudies/authorhome.jsp?authorID=98&collateralID=5303&displayName=Biography>.

Variation: Students can create a postcard to send to family or friends who are dealing with the loss of a pet. Students can write inspirational words to help friends, family, or themselves deal with this tragic event in their lives. Students can send the postcard electronically by accessing the *Electronic Postcards in the Classroom* Web site at <http://eduscapes.com/tap/topic92.htm>.

■ Storyboarding

Information Literacy Standards: 2, 3, 4, 5
NCTE/IRA Standards for English Language Arts: 1, 3, 11, 12

After reading the text, students can practice the skill of sequencing by using the Story Board strategy (Tompkins, 2003). Make the storyboards by cutting apart two copies of the text/picture book and gluing the pages on tag board to make them sturdy. Laminating the storyboards is suggested. To practice sequencing, line the storyboards on a board tray or hang on a clothesline. Students can visualize the story and its structure by examining the text and illustrations. Distribute the pages randomly to students and require students to put them in order by asking them to stand in line.

Steps:

1. Acquire two copies of the book.
2. Cut the books apart and separate the pages.
3. Attach pages to tag board. Laminate, if desired.
4. Pass out storyboard or line board ledge with storyboards for sequencing activities.

Human Dog Year Chart

Directions: Interview family and friends and write their age in the Human Years column then convert the age to Dog Years. Write the Dog Year in the second column; be sure to show your work in column two. **One Human year is equal to seven dog years.** Complete the third column by doing a subtraction problem. An example is provided.

Human Years	Dog Years	What is the difference?
Example: Carlos is 5 years old.	*In dog years, Carlos is 35 years old. (7 x 5 = 35) (Hint: multiply dog years by human years)*	*35 - 5 = 30 (Subtract dog years from from human years to get the difference)*

Human Dog Year Chart. Figure 6.2

Postcard Template

Dear: _____

_____

_____

_____

_____

_____

_____

_____

_____

_____

_____

_____

_____

Front

U.S. MAIL

Back

Postcard Template. Figure 6.3

Beyond the Text: Lesson Extensions

■ **Memory Books**

Information Literacy Standards: 1, 2, 3, 4, 5
NCTE/IRA Standards for English Language Arts: 4, 5, 6, 8, 11, 12

Using pictures of the children's favorite pets, make a memory book of the pet as a keepsake. Use construction paper and bind it with string or ribbon. Inside the book students can design pages of happy memories with their pets. Students can decorate the cover with stickers, trinkets, pictures, or embellishments. It is important that the memory book is personal and reflects their individuality. For additional information on making the memory book, visit the following Web sites: <www.scrapbook.lifetips.com> and <www.brainbetty.com/scrapbooking.htm>. For students who do not have pets, have them visit the following Web sites to collect pictures of dachshunds like Elfie, the dog portrayed in the story: <www.akc.org/breeds/dachshund/index.cfm> or <www.doxieskennel.com/>. Students can create a memory book centered on Elfie as the subject for their memory book.

The Tenth Good Thing About Barney

Copyright date: 1971
Author: Judith Viorst
Recommended age range: four to nine

Discovery and Discussion: Setting the Stage for Reading

Summary

After his beloved cat, Barney, dies, a young boy tries to make sense of his loss by listing the ten best things about his adored pet.

Words for Review: died, funeral, brace

■ Life Cycle

Information Literacy Standards: 3, 4
NCTE/IRA Standards for English Language Arts: 4, 11, 12

To help students comprehend the story, discuss and explain the cycle of life components.

■ Plant a Flower Seed

Have each student plant their own seed to make connections to the plot of the story.

Materials:

- Styrofoam cups
- Seeds
- Planting soil
- Markers
- Water

Steps:

1. Allow students to decorate their cup as a flowerpot.
2. Fill each cup 3/4 full with planting soil.
3. Insert seed.
4. Fill the cup the remainder of the way.
5. Water seeds.

■ Vocabulary Development

Information Literacy Standards: 3, 5, 9
NCTE/IRA Standards for English Language Arts: 11, 12

Review terms from the story before reading to help students better comprehend the story. These terms include: pussywillow tree, orangeade, funeral, and handsome.

Exploration: During Reading

■ Three-Minute Pause

Information Literacy Standards: 2, 3, 4, 5
NCTE/IRA Standards for English Language Arts: 1, 3, 4, 11, 12

Developed by McTighe & Lyman (1988), the Three Minute Pause helps students comprehend the material by taking a break and analyzing what they are reading. The premise is to read or have students read for three minutes, stop, and do the following: 1) summarize the key points so far in the text, 2) add your own thoughts, and 3) pose clarifying questions. By utilizing this strategy, students can successfully process text *while* they are reading as opposed to *after* reading. This strategy will assist students in making connections to their own background knowledge as well as learning from their peers.

■ Ten Good Things

Information Literacy Standards: 2, 3, 4, 5, 9
NCTE/IRA Standards for English Language Arts: 3, 4, 5, 11, 12

For students who have a pet, ask them to make a list of the ten good things about their own pet. For those students who do not have a pet, ask them to list what they believe would be good about owning a pet. Compare their list to the list in the story. The Compare/Contrast Diagram in Figure 6.4 on page 106 can be used for this activity.

Reading Between the Lines: Post Reading

■ Language Experience Approach

Information Literacy Standards: 2, 3, 4, 5, 9
NCTE/IRA Standards for English Language Arts: 3, 4, 11, 12

Language Experience Approach (LEA) (Ashton-Warner, Lee & Allen, 1963, Stauffer, 1970) is a strategy that requires students to dictate words and sentences about their experiences. Act as the "scribe" or secretary for the students by writing what students dictate. As you write, it is important to model how written language works. The student created text becomes the reading material for the day/week. The connection between conventional reading and writing is essential for students' literacy growth.

Steps:

1. Read the story to the students; this text will serve as the stimulus for writing.
2. Talk about the text with students to generate words and review what was read in preparation for writing. This discussion is an opportunity to extend their understanding of the text and vocabulary.
3. Record students' words on chart paper in conventional language, but preserve "their" language as much as possible.
4. Read the text aloud to students, pointing to each word.
5. To extend the experience, ask students to draw pictures to accompany the text.
6. Make sentence strips of the text to keep in a learning center so students can manipulate the text when they practice reading it again and again (Hint: Make individual sentence strips for students by using index cards or tag board).

Compare Contrast Diagram

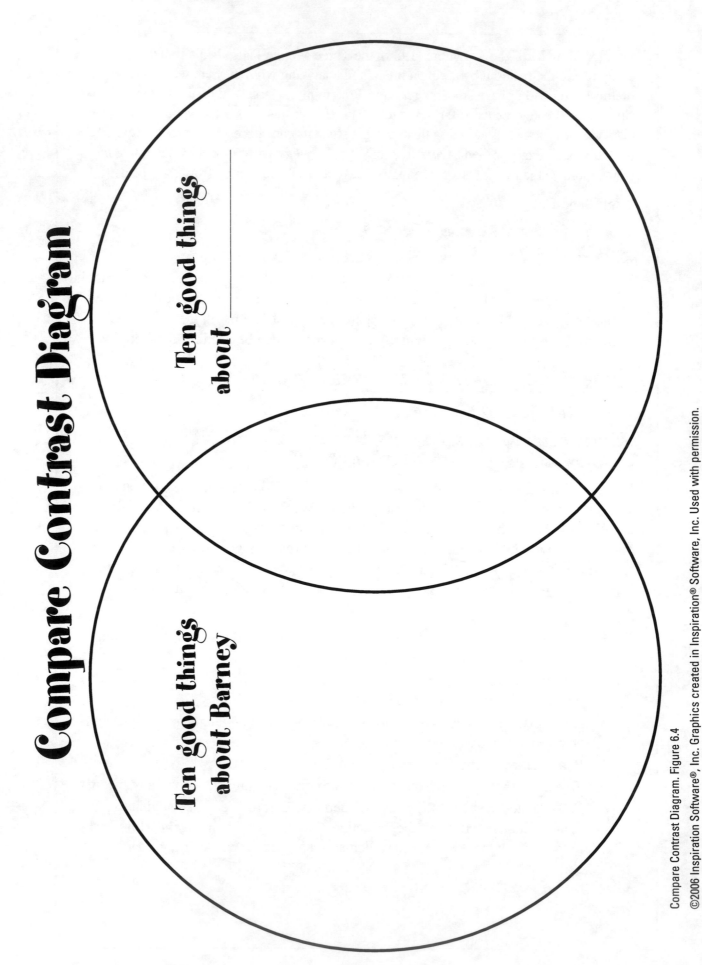

Ten good things about _____

Ten good things about Barney

Compare Contrast Diagram. Figure 6.4

©2006 Inspiration Software®, Inc. Graphics created in Inspiration® Software, Inc. Used with permission.

Cat Angel Template

Cat Angel Template. Figure 6.5

Beyond the Text: Lesson Extensions

■ **Bereavement Boxes**

Information Literacy Standards: 3, 4, 5
NCTE/IRA Standards for English Language Arts: 4, 11, 12

Using shoeboxes, students can make a Bereavement Box for their pet. Students can decorate the boxes and place pictures, poems, or other trinkets in the box as a way to remember their lost pet. Students can then share these boxes with classmates and family members.

■ **Cat Angel Tree**

Using a bulletin board, the class develops a class Cat Angel Tree. Students can create their own cat angel ornaments to be displayed on the tree. Ornaments can be made from any material including paper. A Cat Angel Template is provided in Figure 6.5 on page 107.

■ **Poetry Activity**

Share the poem *Rainbow Bridge* that can be found on the Web at <www.petloss.com/poems/maingrp/rainbowb.htm>. Follow with discussion.

Additional Book Selections, Professional Resources, and Web Connections on Death of a Pet

Abley, Mark. *Ghost Cat*. Groundwood Books, 2001. Ages five-eight.
An elderly Miss Wilkinson is faced with the loss of her black cat, Tommy Douglas. She buries Tommy Douglas under a rosebush. One day, the rosebush has bloomed with brilliant orange flowers, the color of the cat's eyes. She believes this is a sign from the cat.

Biale, Rachel. *My Pet Died: A Let's Make a Book About It Book*. Tricycle Press, 1997. Ages K-three.
This book is part of the "Let's Make a Book About It" series in which children can make a scrapbook by writing and drawing pictures to express their feelings about the loss of their pet.

Bostrom, Kathleen Long. *The Day Scooter Died: A Book About the Death of a Pet*. Zonderkidz, 2005. Ages K-three.
Mikey's pet, Scooter, dies. Mikey wants to know what has happened to him.

Brown, Margaret Wise. *The Dead Bird*. William Morrow, 2006. Ages five-eight.
Children find a dead bird in the woods and give it a proper burial.

Carrick, Carol. *The Accident*. Houghton Mifflin, 1981. Ages five-eight.
Christopher takes his dog, Bodger, for a walk in the country. Bodger is hit by a truck and killed. Christopher must now deal with the tragedy and get over his guilt. The sequel, *The Foundling,* continues the story as Christopher deals with his feelings of depression and guilt when his parents want him to adopt a new puppy. School Library Journal and International Reading Association Children's Choice Award.

Clark, Emma Chichester. *Up in Heaven*. Doubleday/Random House Children's Books, 2004. Ages five to eight.

> Daisy, the dog, dies in this non-denominational look at heaven and the afterlife. Daisy looks after her former master, Arthur, who in turn helps him find a new puppy.

Cohen, Miriam. *Jim's Dog Muffins*. Yearling, 1986. Ages five-eight.

> Jim's dog, Muffins, has died. His classmates offer sympathy, but Jim is unfriendly until his friend, Paul, helps him find peace. This book presents a realistic picture of Jim's feelings and demeanor in dealing with his loss.

Cullen, Lynn. *The Mightiest Heart*. Dial, 2003. Ages five-eight.

> The retelling of a Welsh legend about Prince Llywelyn and his loyal dog Gelert, who is wrongly banished when the prince believes that Gelert has attacked his son. A multicultural selection.

Dalpra-Berman, Gina. *Remembering Pets: A Book for Children Who Have Lost a Friend*. Robert D. Reed Publishers, 2001. Ages K-three.

> In rhyme form this book helps children reminisce about the happy times spent with their favorite bird, dog, cat, turtle, and other creatures.

David, Christine. *For Every Dog an Angel*. Lighthearted Press, 2004. Ages five-eight.

> Similar to *For Every Cat an Angel,* this book helps children to think about their feelings concerning their departed pet dog.

Demas, Corinne. *Saying Goodbye to Lulu*. Little, Brown, 2004. Ages five-seven.

> A girl cares for her old black and white mutt, Lulu, whose health is failing and finally dies. Through this first person narrative the girl expresses her feelings. As the story ends, she meets a new puppy.

DiSalvo-Ryan, DyAnne. *A Dog Like Jack*. Holiday House, 1999. Ages five-seven.

> Mike's family adopts a dog, Jack, from a shelter who becomes a precious member of the family. When Jack dies, the boy has the desire to adopt another dog, but expresses that "there will never be another dog like Jack." The epilogue, "Losing a Pet," offers suggestions for coping with pet loss.

Garland, Michael. *Angel Cat*. Boyds Mills Press, 1998. Ages four-seven.

> Matthew and Gillian have two cats, Yin and Yang. A car kills the orange cat, Yin. The children's mother tells them that Yin is now an angel. One night a fire breaks out in the house and Yin flies upstairs to alert the family. Only Matthew and Yang can see Yin, the cat angel who they believe protected them.

Harris, Robie H. *Goodbye Mousie*. Simon, 2001. Ages four-seven.

> An unnamed little boy is sad, angry, and in denial because he can't get his pet mouse to wake up. His father gently tells him that Mousie is dead. Together they paint a box to bury Mousie.

Heckert, Connie. *Dribbles*. Clarion, 1993. Ages five-eight.

> Dribbles, an elderly cat, and her master, a recently widowed old man, move into a new home where three other cats reside. Dribbles is antisocial at first, but she finally makes friends with the other cats. Dribbles dies knowing the other cats loved her.

Hill, Frances. *Bug Cemetery*. Henry Holt, 2002. Ages K-three.

> A boy and his sister, Wilma, hold a pretend funeral for a dead ladybug. Other

neighborhood friends join in by bringing various bugs for burial and create a cemetery. The story takes a turn when Billy's cat is hit by a car and dies. The children bury the cat with the bugs and plant a memorial butterfly garden around the grave. A multicultural selection.

Howard, Ellen. *Murphy and Kate*. Simon & Schuster, 1995. Ages seven-eleven.
Kate and her dog, Murphy, grew up together and are inseparable. Kate is grief stricken when Murphy dies and pledges she will not forget him.

Hughes, Shirley. *Alfie and the Birthday Surprise*. HarperCollins Children's Books, 1998. Ages five-eight.
Smokey, Bob MacNally's prize cat, dies around the time of Bob's birthday. His daughter, Maureen, cheers her father up with a surprise party and a surprise present, a new kitten.

Ichikawa, Satomi. *My Pig Amarillo*. Philomel, 2003. Ages four-seven.
Pablito's best friend is Amarillo, a yellow pet pig, a gift from his grandfather. Pablito, a Guatemalan boy, and Amarillo become best friends and are inseparable until one day when Amarillo is no longer around. The boy is distraught until Pablito's grandfather finds a way to send a message to the deceased pig. A multicultural selection.

Keller, Holly. *Goodbye Max*. Greenwillow, 1987. Ages four-eight.
Ben's dog, Max, has died. His parents, who Ben blames for Max's death, bring home a new puppy that Ben resents. With the help of his friend, Zach, Ben works through his grief and decides it is time to make friends with the new puppy.

Kirkpatrick, June. *Barn Kitty*. Azro Press, 1999. Ages four-eight.
This true story describes the adventures of a lost kitten that finds a home with a little boy and his family. Eventually, the cat dies and is sorely missed by the family.

Martin, Jacqueline B. *Grandmother Bryant's Pocket*. Houghton Mifflin, 2000. Ages five-nine.
Set in 1787 in Maine, an eight-year-old girl, Sarah, is distraught after her dog, Patches, dies in a barn fire. Sent to live with her grandparents, Sarah overcomes the death of Patches after learning to care for a one-eyed cat.

Newman, Leslea. *The Best Cat in the World*. Eerdmans Books, 2004. Ages four-eight.
A young child named Victor grieves for his pet cat, Charlie, who dies. Victor is able to adopt a new kitten, Shelly, who helps Victor move on.

Owens, Connie S. *Missing Maggie: The Death of a Pet*. Warner, 2003. Ages K-three.
A boy mourns the death of his dog, Maggie.

Pank, Rachel. *Under the Blackberries*. Scholastic, 1992. Ages five-eight.
A car accident claims the life of Sonia's pet cat, Barney. Her parents comfort her by burying Barney in the backyard where Sonia plants a rosebush. A few weeks later, Sonia gets a new kitten but does not forget Barney.

Parker, Marjorie Blaine. *Jasper's Day*. Kids Can Press, 2002. Ages five-eight.
Riley, the young narrator, explains that Jasper, the dog, has cancer and is about to

be euthanized. The family has a celebration in honor of their pet's life.

Puttock, Simon. *Story for Hippo.* Scholastic Press, 2001. Ages five-eight.
Hippo, Chameleon, and Monkey are best friends and enjoy spending time together telling silly jokes and funny stories. One day, old Hippo explains that she is tired and will go off into the jungle's shade to die. Monkey becomes grief-stricken for a long time until Chameleon comforts him.

Rogers, Fred. *When a Pet Dies.* Putnam, 1998. Ages five-eight.
From the First Experience series, this book identifies a child's feelings of sad-ness, loneliness, and frustration over the loss of a pet.

Rosen, Michael. *Bonesy and Isabel.* Harcourt, 1995. Ages K-three.
Isabel, an adopted child from El Salvador who has been adopted by an American family deals with the loss of her pet dog, Old Bonesy. A multicultural selection.

Rylant, Cynthia. *Cat Heaven.* Blue Sky Press, 1997. Ages five-seven.
Similar to Rylant's *Dog Heaven*, whose purpose is to comfort a pet owner who mourns a lost pet, this title with its rhyming text depicts cats that can now fly.

Stewart, Elisabeth Jane. *Bimmi Finds a Cat.* Clarion, 1996. Ages six-ten.
An eight-year-old Creole boy, Bimmi Ladouce, finds his gray cat, Crabmeat, lying dead beside a coconut palm. While still grieving his loss, another cat, Kitty-Louise, befriends him. He takes Kitty-Louise home only to realize that someone may be missing her as much as he misses Crabmeat. He then goes searching for Kitty-Louise's owner and finds new friendship. A multicultural selection.

Stockton, Anne. *Honey-Bun.* Educare Press, 1999. Ages four-seven.
The author shares her pain of losing her cat in this personal memoir format.

Turner, Pamela. *Hachiko: The True Story of a Loyal Dog.* Houghton Mifflin, 2004. Ages five-ten.
Kentaro, a young boy, tells the story of the loyalty Hachiko has to his master. Even after his master, Dr. Ueno has been dead for 10 years, the dog returns everyday to wait for him at Shibuya Station, a train station in Tokyo. Eventually, Hachiko dies. A bronze statue has been built at the Shibuya Station to honor this special canine and a festival is held every April. BCCB Blue Ribbon Picture Book Award. A multicultural selection.

Wittbold, Maureen. *Mending Peter's Heart.* Portunus Publishing, 1995. Ages K-three.
Peter goes through the grieving process when his husky dog, Mishka, dies.

Zolotow, Charlotte. *My Old Dog.* HarperCollins, 1995. Ages four-eight.
This revered author tells the story of Ben and his dog who was his best friend until the dog passes on. The story ends with a happy ending of Ben's parents bringing home a new puppy. A multicultural selection.

Professional Resources

Carmack, Betty J. *Grieving the Death of a Pet.* Augsburg Fortress Publishers, 2003.
The author draws on personal experiences as well as interviews of other pet owners who have dealt with pet loss.

Greene, Lorrie and Jacquelyn Landis. *Saying Good-Bye to the Pet You Love: A Complete Resource to Help You Heal.* New Harbinger Publications, 2002.
Written by a psychologist with twenty years of experience as a pet-bereavement specialist, this book shares many strategies for families grieving the loss of a pet. A chapter on explaining the pet's death to a child is especially helpful.

Heegaard, Marge. *Saying Goodbye to Your Pet: Children Can Learn to Cope with Grief.* Fairview, 2001.
This book for children depicts coping with the loss of a pet through art therapy.

Johnston, Marianne. *Let's Talk About When Your Pet Dies.* Powerkids Press, 1998.
This book explains the feelings that one may experience when a pet dies and discusses how to cope with these feelings.

Kowalski, Gary. *Goodbye, Friend: Healing Wisdom for Anyone Who Has Ever Lost a Pet.* Stillpoint Publishing, 1997.
The title describes the content of this book that includes ideas for rituals, ceremonies, readings and poems to use for coping with the loss of a pet.

Nieburg, Herbert. *Pet Loss: Thoughtful Guide for Adults and Children*, Harper, 1996.
This handbook offers advice and strategies for pet owners who have suffered the loss of a pet. A chapter entitled, "How can children be helped with their grief over the death of a family pet," provides insight on handling this sensitive issue.

Stuparyk, Emily Margaret. *When Only the Love Remains: The Pain of Pet Loss.* Hushion House, 2000.
This personal narrative is written in journal format and expresses the author's sadness through poetry.

Wolfert, Alan D. *When Your Pet Dies: A Guide to Mourning, Remembering and Healing.* Companion Press, 2004.
This guidebook can be used to help children deal with the trauma associated with losing a pet.

Web Connections

Brookfield Zoo
<www.brookfieldzoo.org/page gen/pretemp4.asp?page id=604&template=4&title=Explore!%20Nature%20Activities%20-%20Pets%20% 20Death%20of%20Pet&bgtype=BgColor&bg=&uni=0&motifid=2000002&form=0 &nsection=&nlinkid=&anchor>
A Brookfield Zoo Web site nature activity dealing with the death of a pet. Honor a pet that has died by creating a memorial for the ebulletin board in the "Zoo at Home" section in the Hamill Family Play Zoo. This section also contains books and a computer station that include information on pets and death.

Care for Animals
<www.avma.org/careforanimals/animatedjourneys/goodbyefriend/goodbye.asp>
　　Created by the American Veterinary Medical Association, this handy site
　　containing researched-based information dealing with pet loss.

Children and Pet Loss
<http://griefhealing.com/childrenandpetloss.htm>
　　This site presents an extensive list of links in categories such as general pet loss,
　　children and pet loss, missing pets, pet loss articles and booklists.

Dougy Center for Grieving Children
　　Grieving families can find support in a safe, caring way and can share their
　　experiences as they move through their grief process.

Grieving the Loss of a Pet
<www.helpguide.org/life/grieving_pets.htm>
　　A selection of researched-based articles dealing with children's feelings in regard to
　　death of a pet and the stages of grief they may experience is presented on this site.

Kids and Pets
<www.kidsaid.com/knp.html>
　　Children will enjoy using this useful, kid-friendly site largely collected from pet
　　e-zines on caring for pets.

Tears Fill the Void After the Death of a Pet
<www.cvm.uiuc.edu/petcolumns/showarticle.cfm?id=148>
　　From the College of Veterinary Medicine in Urbana, Illinois, this site offers
　　practical ideas for helping children deal with pet loss.

Chapter 7

Adoption

Tell Me Again About the Night I Was Born

Copyright date: 1996
Author: Jamie Lee Curtis
Recommended age range: four to eight

Discovery and Discussion: Setting the Stage for Reading

- **Words for Review:** adoption, happy tears, lullaby, family

- **Vocabulary Builder**

  Information Literacy Standards: 1, 3, 4, 9
  NCTE/IRA Standards for English Language Arts: 1, 3, 4, 5, 8, 11, 12

Summary

This true adoption story by Jamie Lee Curtis conveys the love adoptive parents feel for their new baby. Love, affection, and comfort of family take center stage of the text and portrays that love for a child is unconditional. This story emphasizes the importance of knowing the definition of family, which sits at the forefront of this story.

Before reading this story, discuss important vocabulary terms such as *adoption*, *family*, *lullaby*, and *happy tears*. Brainstorm what students think these terms and concepts mean. Ask students to depict in words and pictures their definition of family and display their creations emphasizing that family means different things to different people. Depictions can be hand drawn, collages, or clipart from the computer. Ask students to share their creations with the class so that they can see and hear the different versions of what a family is. Students can then identify that being a part of any family makes them unique and special.

■ Concept Mapping

Information Literacy Standards: 4, 5, 9
NCTE/IRA Standards for English Language Arts: 11, 12

Ask students to identify the attributes and qualities of the word adoption. Record students' responses on a class concept map that can be hung on the wall. Revisit and revise the concept map during the post reading segment. This process allows students to visually connect with the terminology during the reading of the text and completion of activities.

■ Family Connection

Information Literacy Standards: 3, 4, 5
NCTE/IRA Standards for English Language Arts: 4, 9, 11, 12

Make copies of Figure 7.1, Family Interview on page 117. Ask students to interview their own parents/guardians/grandparents about the "night" they were born. This procedure assists students in making personal connections to the text as well as notice similarities and differences to their own birthday. Students share their stories that can eventually be made into their own storybook. For younger children, ask parents/guardians to complete the form and return it. The librarian/school library media specialist or teachers can write the text while the students illustrate the storybook pages.

Exploration: During Reading

Discussion after each page may be necessary while guiding students to a true understanding of the concept of adoption. When necessary, stop and discuss what students are learning about adoption and add the information to the class concept map.

Reading Between the Lines: Post Reading

■ Revision/Revisiting the Concept Map

Information Literacy Standards: 4, 5, 9
NCTE/IRA Standards for English Language Arts: 1, 11, 12

After reading the text, revisit the whole class concept map and add information based on the students' interpretation of the text.

■ Checking for Comprehension: Discussion Questions

Information Literacy Standards: 4, 5, 7, 9
NCTE/IRA Standards for English Language Arts: 1, 3, 4, 11, 12

Discuss the following questions with students:
1. What did the main character's mother do the first night she was a mommy? How is this similar or different from your experience?
2. What is a lullaby? Can you name a lullaby that you have heard before? Share popular lullabies with students.

 # Family Interview

Directions: Choose a family member to interview. Ask the following questions and write the answers in the spaces provided.

What day was I born? (i.e.: Monday) _____

What month, day, and year was I born? _____

What time was I born? _____

What was the weather like when I was born? _____

What was the name of the hospital in
which I was born? _____

Who was present when I was born? _____

Tell me about your visit to the nursery to see me for the first time:

_____

_____

_____

Tell me about our first night as a family:

_____

_____

_____

What songs/lullabies did you sing to me when I was born?

_____

_____

_____

Attach a newborn picture, if possible.

Additional Information:

_____

_____

_____

Family Interview. Figure 7.1

■ Music Connection

Teach children to sing a lullaby. After students learn the words, they can add hand motions.

■ Skill Builder: Similes (grades two and up)

Information Literacy Standards: 3, 6, 9
NCTE/IRA Standards for English Language Arts: 3, 4, 5, 6, 11, 12

On page 20 Curtis writes, "Tell me again how you carried me like a china doll all the way home and how you glared at anyone who sneezed." Point out the words "like a china doll" in the text and provide students with the definition of a simile. Share additional examples to reinforce the concept. Other examples to share include: sly as a fox, red as a cherry, busy as a bee. Ask students to complete the following simile sentences:

1. The scarf was as _____ as a _____.
2. The snow was as _____ as a _____.
3. My nose was as red as a (n) _____.

A mini-lesson on syntax can be taught at this time. An important skill to teach is the skill of predicting what may come next in a sentence. If "a" is before the blank, the word must start with a consonant, if "an" comes before the blank, students use a word that starts with a vowel. For example, my nose was as red as an apple.

Guide students through the process of writing their own "secret similes."

1. Write a noun on the board.
2. Ask students to describe the teacher. Ask questions to support students such as "how big?" or "what kind?" Continue this procedure until students have a description.
3. Ask students to pair up with a work partner.
4. Each student is given a blank piece of drawing paper. Instruct students to write their name on the top of the paper. Ask students to write a noun at the top of the paper without showing anyone.
5. Students pass the paper to another student who writes the description on the paper.
6. The paper is passed to a third person who writes the simile sentence using the noun and description.
7. The paper is passed to a fourth person who illustrates the simile.
8. Do not allow students to discuss their creations. Papers are returned to its owner for viewing. Students then share their papers that were created by four unique people in the class.

Beyond the Text: Lesson Extensions

■ Family Storybooks (adaptations provided for younger children)

Information Literacy Standards: 1, 2, 3, 4, 6, 9
NCTE/IRA Standards for English Language Arts: 1, 3, 4, 5, 6, 7, 11, 12

Using the Family Interview guide (Figure 7.1) completed earlier, students can create their own picture book about the "night" they were born. Encourage older students to include similes in their text as well. Allow students to share their books by reading them aloud to classmates before presenting the books to their parents/guardians. Display the books in the library and allow other children to "check them out" during independent reading time. For younger children, it may be necessary to write the text and allow them to illustrate the storybook. Ask parents/guardians to assist by writing the text for the children or by typing using a word processing program. Illustrations can also be created using clipart or the paint program on the computer.

■ Diorama

Information Literacy Standards: 1, 3, 4, 5, 6, 9
NCTE/IRA Standards for English Language Arts: 1, 3, 4, 5, 6, 11, 12

Students create a diorama of their favorite scene from the book. A diorama is a three dimensional scene that is made by placing objects in front of a background. A shoebox is typically used for this miniature scene display.

Steps:

1. Students choose a favorite scene from the book to create their diorama.

2. Students decide how the backdrop will be depicted. If the scene took place outside in the woods, for example, the students may paint an outdoor scene consisting of trees, the sky, birds, while an indoor scene may include wallpaper, windows, or doors. Allow students to use paint on their box for this step.

3. The outside of the box should also be decorated to reflect their theme. Paint, wallpaper, or construction paper works well on the outside. Students can write the title and author of the book on the outside of the box.

4. The three dimensional scene is then created. Students can create characters from paper or clay. Figures are often used to depict characters if they have these materials at home. The goal is to make the scene seem as realistic as possible.

5. Glue all standing objects securely to the box.

6. For older students: Require older students to write a two-paragraph explanation of what is happening in the scene they portrayed. A summary of the book may also be added to the writing. Grade the paragraphs on content, mechanics, creativity, and neatness.

Stellaluna

Copyright date: 1993
Author: Janell Cannon
Recommended age range: five to nine
Awards: American Bookseller Book of the Year Award, Publishers Weekly Children's Bestseller, Reading Rainbow Feature and Review Book, Keystone to Reading Book Award, Southern California Council on Literature for Young People Award

Discovery and Discussion: Setting the Stage for Reading

- **Words for Review:** fruit bat, peculiar, embarrassing, perched

Summary

Stellaluna, a baby bat, finds herself in a nest with baby birds when an owl attacks her mother. Stellaluna is welcomed into her new family only if she can act like a bird. Soon, Stellaluna introduces her new siblings to the world of bats. They are confused by the concept of being different. This story is appropriate for anyone who has left the "nest" only to realize we are all more alike than we may think.

- **KWL**

> Information Literacy Standards: 1, 2, 3, 4, 5, 6, 9
> NCTE/IRA Standards for English Language Arts: 1, 3, 4, 7, 11, 12

Prior to reading *Stellaluna* complete a KWL (What I Know, What I Want to Know, What I Learned) chart (Ogle, 1986) with students. A KWL Chart is provided in Figure 7.2 on page 121.

Create a large class size chart and ask students to tell you everything they know about bats in the K column. Next, ask students everything they want to know about bats in the W column. Ask students to share their information from the K column and talk about any misconceptions that may exist (The last two pages of the book can be read prior to the storybook. This expository text about bats may be helpful for students' comprehension).

After reading, ask students to complete the L column to discuss what was learned from the text.

- **Real Life Adoption/Mentoring**

> Information Literacy Standards: 1, 9
> NCTE/IRA Standards for English Language Arts: 4, 5, 6, 11, 12

Discuss the concept of adoption with students emphasizing the positives. Inform students they will "adopt" someone in school. For older students you may ask the kindergarten or first grade teacher to team up with you in this adoption endeavor. Younger students may be "adopted" by an older student in the school. Arrange for weekly or biweekly meetings/visits so that students can spend time together engaging in a variety of literacy and mentoring activities. An introductory letter writing activity can be an effective way to begin the process. Letters can be exchanged weekly. When

KWL Chart

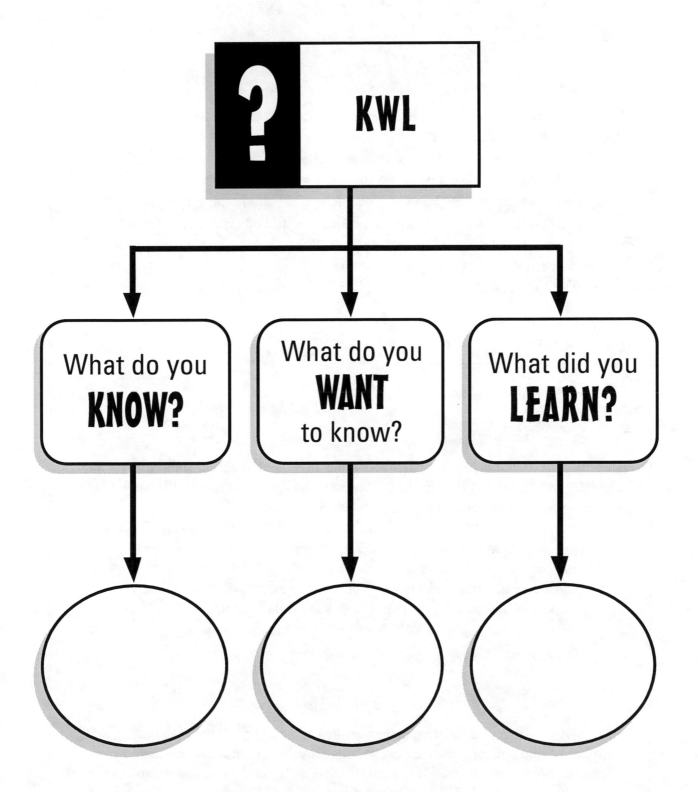

KWL. Figure 7.2

©2006 Inspiration Software®, Inc. Graphics created in Inspiration® Software, Inc. Used with permission.

planning the visits, allow students to help plan the activities as a way to encourage ownership. If this is not an option, consider adopting a class pet.

Exploration: During Reading

■ Checking for Comprehension: Discussion Questions

Information Literacy Standards: 4, 5, 7, 9
NCTE/IRA Standards for English Language Arts: 1, 3, 4, 11, 12

The concept of stereotypes should be a focal point when reading the text. Questions for discussion:

1. Do you think the friendship between Stellaluna and the birds will last? Why/Why not? What obstacles may they encounter? What are these obstacles?
2. What would have happened to Stellaluna if she did not find her mother?
3. Do you think the birds would have tried to act like bats? Why/Why not?
4. What role did the owl play in the story? Did the owl act as you would have suspected?
5. Do you feel differently about bats after reading this text? What are your feelings after reading?

Reading Between the Lines: Post Reading

■ Venn Diagrams

Information Literacy Standards: 1, 2, 3, 9
NCTE/IRA Standards for English Language Arts: 1, 3, 4, 5, 7, 11, 12

After reading *Stellaluna,* have students complete the Venn diagrams in Figures 7.3 on page 123 and Figure 7.4 on page 124. The Bats and Birds diagram in Figure 7.3 is used to compare/contrast bats and birds based on what was learned from the text. Since Stellaluna had the ability to "fit in" with the bird family, students can easily see what these two animals have in common. The You and Friends diagram in Figure 7.4 can be used for a more personal connection with the text. Students compare/contrast themselves with a friend. After students complete the diagrams, ask them to discuss how being unique and different can be positive. Ask students to brainstorm a class list of other people they know that are unique and what makes them unique.

■ Skill Builder: Making Words/Building Words

Information Literacy Standards: 1, 3, 9
NCTE/IRA Standards for English Language Arts: 1, 6, 11, 12

This activity can be used for learning centers. In order to reinforce the skill of vocabulary/word building, use the Letter Cards provided in Figure 7.5 on page 126. Laminate or print on cardstock so the letter cards can be used over time. Instruct students to spread the letters on their desk. Using a timer, ask students to form two-letter words and write the words in the appropriate column on the worksheet. Ask students to

Bats and Birds

BIRDS

BATS

Bats and Birds. Figure 7.3
©2006 Inspiration Software®, Inc. Graphics created in Inspiration® Software, Inc. Used with permission.

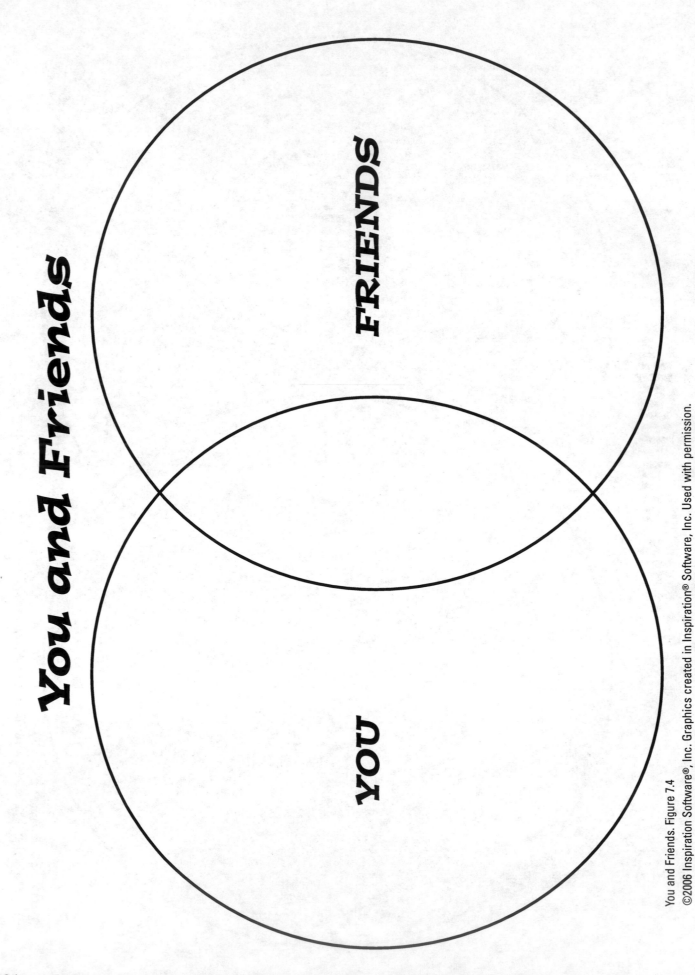

You and Friends. Figure 7.4

©2006 Inspiration Software®, Inc. Graphics created in Inspiration® Software, Inc. Used with permission.

complete three-letter words, four-letter words and so on until they create the ten-letter word, Stellaluna. This practice increases the skills of phonics/phonemic awareness and vocabulary building. Adapt this activity to meet students' cognitive and psychomotor abilities.

Beyond the Text: Lesson Extensions

- **Bat Mobile/Library Research (recommended for grades two and up)**

  Information Literacy Standards: 1, 2, 3, 4, 5, 6, 7, 8, 9
  NCTE/IRA Standards for English Language Arts: 1, 3, 4, 5, 6, 7, 8, 11, 12

Using the information students have already learned about bats as a starting point, assign students to go to the library and research a particular type of bat. Students can use the nonfiction books in the library as well as the Internet. The following Web site from the U.S. Fish and Wildlife Services provides comprehensive information on bats: <www.fws.gov/endangered/bats/bats.htm>. Have students find answers to the following questions:

1. What food does the bat typically eat?
2. Where does the bat live?
3. Where is the bat indigenous? (Where does the bat live?)
4. Describe the bat's specific characteristics.
5. What is the scientific name of the bat?

After students complete their research, students can create a bat mobile. The following materials are needed to create the bat mobile: wire clothes hangers, string or yarn, hole punch, scissors, and the Bat Template in Figure 7.7 on page 128. Reproduce the Bat Template in Figure 7.7 and distribute. Students record the answers from their library research on each bat, cut out each bat, and assemble the bat mobile. Have students share orally their research findings on the bat mobile. Oral presentation rubrics are available at <http://rubistar.4teachers.org/index.php>. Display the bat mobiles in the library, classroom, or hallway.

Letter Cards

I	a
I	u
e	n
t	I
s	a

Letter Cards. Figure 7.5

Making Words, Building Words Worksheet

Name: _____

2 letter words	3 letter words	4 letter words	5 letter words	6 letter words	7 letter words	8 letter words	9 letter words

The ten-letter word that I made is: _____

Making Words, Building Words. Figure 7.6

Bat Template

Bat Template. Figure 7.7

I Love You Like Crazy Cakes

Copyright date: 2000
Author: Rose Lewis
Recommended age range: five to eight

Discovery and Discussion: Setting the Stage for Reading

- **Words for Review:** nannies, hotel, linens, pretended, lullaby

- **Prediction**

Summary

Rose Lewis who went to China to adopt a baby girl, Alexandra Mae-Ming, narrates this true story. This story is about their journey to become a family. This book is a multicultural selection and supports the social studies curriculum standards for studying Asia.

> *Information Literacy Standards: 1, 2, 6, 9*
> *NCTE/IRA Standards for English Language Arts: 3, 4, 11, 12*

Hold up the book. Ask students to study the picture on the front cover. Ask students, "What can you tell about this book by just looking at the cover?" "What do you think the story will be about?"

- **Map Skills**

Secure a world atlas or globe from the library or have students access the following online atlas at <www.atlapedia.com/online/maps/political/China_etc.htm>. Have students locate the country of China on the map. Identify several of the countries that surround China, and find the capital of China, Beijing. Reproduce the map of China in Figure 7.8 on page 130 and have students label it with the surrounding countries. Have students label the compass directions (north, south, east, and west) also.

Exploration: During Reading

- **Discussion**

Stop reading periodically to discuss the new mother's thoughts and feelings.

- **Reading Comprehension/Making Connections**

> *Information Literacy Standards: 3, 6, 9*
> *NCTE/IRA Standards for English Language Arts: 1, 3, 11, 12*

Ask students how the title of the story relates to what happened in the story. Ask students if they think this is an appropriate title for the story. Why/Why not? Go back to the picture on page ten. Ask students to reflect about what is happening in the story.

Reading Between the Lines: Post Reading

- **Chinese Calligraphy**

The last page of this story displays the Chinese pictorial character for the word "love." Explain to students that the Chinese language is written using over 50,000

Map of China

Directions: Label the following items on the map: 1) compass directions (north, south, east, and west); 2) the capital of China; and 3) the countries that surround China.

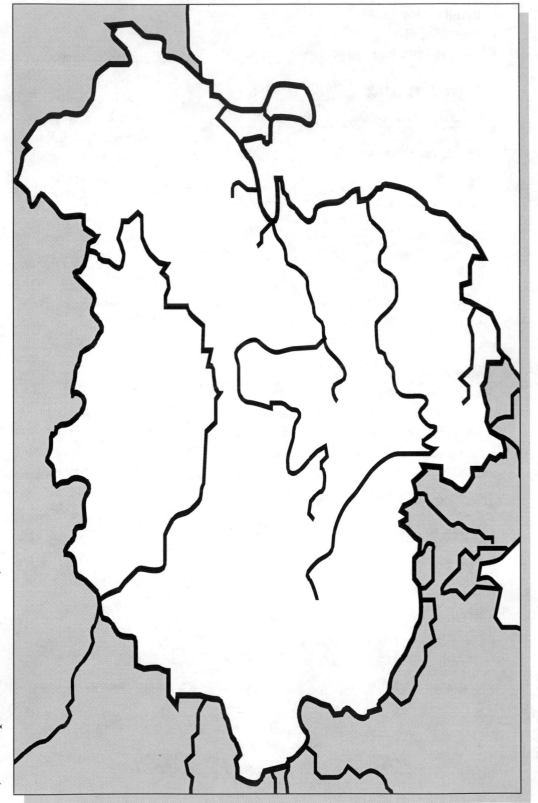

Map of China. Figure 7.8

Chinese characters and to read and understand a typical Chinese newspaper, a person would need to know about 4,000 characters. The art of forming the characters is called calligraphy. Have students visit the Web site, <http://formosa-translation.com/names/> to try their hand at calligraphy by spelling their name in Chinese. Students' name calligraphy can be displayed in the library or classroom.

■ Route to China (grades two and up)

Information Literacy Standards: 1, 2, 3, 4, 5, 8, 9
NCTE/IRA Standards for English Language Arts: 1, 3, 4, 5, 6, 7, 8, 11, 12

Provide students with world atlases from the library and review skills for using an atlas. As an alternative, have students access one of the following Web sites: <http://encarta.msn.com/encnet/features/MapCenter/map.aspx> or <http://plasma.nationalgeographic.com/mapmachine/>. Ask them to write a detailed, step-by-step set of directions telling how to get from the United States to China traveling east to west by land and sea, as the author of this story did. The starting point should be Boston, Massachusetts, home of the author.

For older students have them share observations from local and long distance travel using tele-fieldtrips on the Web. Use the Adventure Online Web site available at <www.adventureonline.com>.

■ Recipe for Crazy Cakes

Information Literacy Standards: 3, 5, 9
NCTE/IRA Standards for English Language Arts: 4, 5, 6, 11, 12

Using a whole class team approach, compose a recipe for crazy cakes. Students will decide what ingredients are in crazy cakes and how to make this treat. It can be as simple or crazy as the students want. After the recipe is written, use the Language Experience Approach (page 149) to write an explanatory paragraph detailing how the crazy cakes are prepared.

■ Acrostic Poem Quilt

Information Literacy Standards: 3, 5, 9
NCTE/IRA Standards for English Language Arts: 4, 5, 6, 11, 12

Using the words *Crazy Cakes*, students create an acrostic poem to reflect the character traits of the main character in the text. Students are required to use descriptive adjectives when writing their poems to illustrate their comprehension of the story in this creative acrostic poem. After a final draft of each poem is either hand written or typed on the word processor, require students to mount the poem on construction paper and decorate as they like. Make a class paper quilt by taping or stapling all poems together. Display the quilt in the library, classroom, or hallway. Students can also use the following Web site to create their poem electronically: <www.readwritethink.org/materials/acrostic/>.

Beyond the Text: Lesson Extensions

■ Chinese Population
Explain that China is the world's largest country in population, with approximately one fifth of the world's people. Have students use a current almanac from the library or an online almanac available at <www.worldalmanacforkids.com/explore/index.html> or <www.infoplease.com/almanacs.html> to check the latest estimates for the population of the world, China, and the United States. First, have students make a pie graph that shows the percentage of the world's population who are Chinese. Second, have students make a bar graph to compare and illustrate the population of China and the population of the United States. Graphs can be generated using the *Microsoft Excel*™ program. For younger students, this lesson can be completed as a whole group.

■ Chinese Numbers
Explain the Chinese have over 50,000 characters that make up their language. Have students access the following Web site on Chinese numbers: <www.edhelper.com/ChineseNumbers.htm>. Have students practice writing the Chinese character for the numbers zero through 10. Conclude by having students write math problems with these characters and share them with the class.

■ Guest Speaker/Electronic Appearance
Invite a guest speaker of Chinese heritage or someone who has traveled to China recently to speak to the class about Chinese celebrations, traditions, and customs. (Hint: If possible and with permission of the speaker, videotape the presentation for future use.) Have students write a summary of what they learned from the speaker about the Chinese culture.

As an alternative to having a speaker in person, arrange for a guest speaker through a videocast or Webcast using the CU-SeeMe program available through Cornell University's CU-SeeMe Page at <www.webopedia.com/TERM/C/CU_SeeMe.html> or use Classroom Conferencing Online from the Global School Network at <www.gsn.org/gsh/cu/index.html>.

■ Electronic Pen Pals: ePals
Electronic pen pals or key pals promote cross-cultural learning and enable literacy practice. Arrange for students to have an electronic pen pal. The ePals Chinese-English Language and Learning Portal is one of the latest initiative to partner Chinese and native English speaking classrooms worldwide for Chinese and English language learning. Further information is available at <www.epals.com/projects/chinaportal/>.

■ Make a Passport

Information Literacy Standards: 3, 5, 9
NCTE/IRA Standards for English Language Arts: 4, 5, 6, 11, 12

Explain that in order to travel to other countries, a passport is a necessary travel document. Have students create their own passports using the Passport Cover Figure 7.9 on

Passport Cover

Photo:

UNITED STATES
of AMERICA

This passport is issued to:

_____
(your name)

Issue Date: _____

Birthdate: _____

Place of Birth: _____

Country: _____

Passport Cover. Figure 7.9

page 133. Use the digital camera to take students' pictures and paste them on the cover. Older students can visit the United States Government's Web site, <http://travel.state.gov/ passport/passport_1738.html> and read the information on passports. Have students write a paragraph on what information is contained in a passport and why it is necessary to have a passport.

■ First Person Narrative

Information Literacy Standards: 2, 3, 4
NCTE/IRA Standards for English Language Arts: 4, 5, 6, 11, 12

I Love You Like Crazy Cakes is written in first-person. The mother tells her daughter the journey taken to become a family. Ask students to brainstorm a story they would like to share with someone special in their lives. Using the writing process, require students to write a first-person narrative of their own. Outline writing criteria that are developmentally appropriate for students. Writing rubrics are available at <http://rubistar.4teachers.org/index.php>. Students can share these stories as a read aloud in the library, classroom, or as an open house project.

Additional Book Selections, Professional Resources, and Web Connections on Adoption

Bang, Molly. *In My Heart.* Little, Brown, 2006. Ages five-seven.
  Parents describe how their child is always in their hearts, no matter where they are or what they are doing. Caldecott author.

Banish, Roslyn. *A Forever Family.* Harper Collins, 1992. Ages six-eight.
  A different viewpoint of *I Love You Like Crazy Cakes,* this true account of a young Chinese girl relates how it feels to be part of an adoptive family in America but still be proud of her Chinese heritage. A multicultural listing.

Bond, Juliet C. *Sam's Sister.* Perspectives, 2004. Ages five-eight.
  This picture book deals with the emotional aspects of adjusting to the difficult reality of giving up a child for adoption. A multicultural selection.

Brodzinski, Anne Braff. *The Mulberry Bird: An Adoption Story.* Perspectives, 1996. Ages seven-nine.
  Although she loves her baby very much, a young mother bird gives him up for adoption because she is unable to give him the home that he needs.

Ching, Tokie. *A Hawaii Japanese New Year with Yuki-chan.* Mutual, 2003. Ages five-eight.
  Yuki-chan prepares for the Japanese New Year with her adopted family. A multicultural selection.

Cole, Joanna. *How I Was Adopted.* HarperTrophy, 1999. Ages five-eight.
  A young girl tells the story of how she came to be her parents' child through adoption. Award winning author.

Curtis, Christopher Paul. *Bud, Not Buddy.* Yearling, 2002. Ages nine-twelve.
  Ten-year-old Bud, a motherless boy living in Flint, Michigan, during the Great

Depression, escapes a bad foster home and sets out in search of the man he believes to be his father—the renowned bandleader, H.E. Calloway of Grand Rapids. A multicultural selection. Newbery Award. Corretta Scott King Author Award.

Friedrich, Molly. *You're Not My Real Mother*. Little, Brown, 2004. Ages five-eight. After an adoptive mother tells her daughter all the reasons that she is her "real mother," the young girl realizes that her mother is right, even though they do not look alike.

Giff, Patricia. *The Pictures of Hollis Woods*. Random House, 2004. Ages eight-twelve. A troublesome twelve-year-old orphan, staying with an elderly artist who needs her, remembers the only other time she was happy in a foster home, with a family that truly seemed to care about her. Newbery and Boston Globe-Horn Book Author.

Girard, Linda Walvoord. *Adoption Is for Always*. A. Whitman, 1991. Ages five-eight. Although Celia reacts to having been adopted with anger and insecurity, her parents help her accept her feelings and celebrate their love for her by making her adoption day a family holiday. Includes factual information about the adoption process.

Girard, Linda Walvoord. *We Adopted You, Benjamin Koo*. A. Whitman, 1989. Ages seven-eleven.
Nine-year-old Benjamin Koo Andrews, adopted from Korea as an infant, describes what it is like to grow up adopted from another country. A multicultural selection.

Gray, Kes. *Our Twitchy*. Holt, 2003. Ages five-seven.
Twitchy, a young bunny, realizes his parents, a cow and a horse, do not look like him. He must come to terms with the idea that they are still his "real" parents.

Harrar, George. *Parents Wanted*. Milkweed, 2001. Ages eight-twelve.
Twelve-year-old Andrew, who has ADD, is adopted by new parents after years of other foster homes and desperately hopes that he will not mess up the situation.

Ibbotson, Eva. *The Star of Kazan*. Dutton, 2004. Ages nine-twelve.
Reminiscent of classics such as *Heidi* and *Sara Crewe*, this story portrays Annika, abandoned as an infant but later adopted by two loving "aunts," who dreams of meeting her real mother. The story is set against early twentieth century Vienna. A multicultural selection. Pennsylvania School Library Association Best of the Best Children's Book Award, 2004.

Kasza, Keiko. *A Mother for Choco*. Puffin, 1992. Ages five-seven.
A lonely little bird named Choco goes in search of a mother.

Katz, Karen. *Over the Moon*. Henry Holt, 1997. Ages five-seven.
A loving couple dream of a baby born far away and know that this is the baby they have been waiting to adopt.

Keller, Holly. *Horace*. Greenwillow, 1991. Ages five-eight.
Horace, a spotted leopard, wonders why he does not look like his parents, who are striped.

Lamperti, Noelle. *Brown Like Me*. New Victoria, 2000. Ages five-eight.
A little girl named Noelle tells how she likes to go looking for things that are brown like her. A multicultural selection.

Lears, Laurie. *Megan's Birthday Tree: A Story About Open Adoption*. A. Whitman, 2005. Ages five-nine.

Every year on Megan's birthday, her birth mother, Kendra, sends a picture of the tree she planted the day Megan was born. When Kendra decides to get married and move to a new house, Megan worries that she will be forgotten.

Little, Jean. *Emma's Yucky Brother*. HarperTrophy, 2000. Ages six-eight.

An older sibling describes what it is like to adjust to a new family.

Livingston, Carole. *Why Was I Adopted?* Lyle Stuart, 1997. Ages five-eight.

Readers will welcome this simple explanation of the facts of adoption.

McCutcheon, John. *Happy Adoption Day*. Little, Brown, 1996. Ages five-eight.

Parents celebrate the day on which they adopted their child and continue to reassure the new addition to their family that it is wanted, loved, and very special.

McMahon, Patricia and Conor Clarke McCarthy. *Just Add One Chinese Sister: An Adoption Story*. Boyds Mills Press, 2005. Ages five-eight.

In this true story, an American family adopts a Chinese girl. A multicultural selection.

Mosher, Richard. *Zazoo*. Houghton Mifflin, 2004. Ages eight-twelve.

Amid old secrets revealed and rifts healed, a thirteen-year-old Vietnamese orphan raised in rural France by her aging "Grand-Pierre" learns about life, death, and love.

Pellegrini, Nina. *Families Are Different*. Holiday House, 1991. Ages five-eight.

An adopted Korean girl discovers that her classmates have different types of families. A multicultural selection.

Rogers, Fred. *Let's Talk About It: Adoption*. Putnam, 1998. Ages five-eight.

Rogers discusses what it means to be part of a family and examines feelings that adopted children may have.

Rosenberg, Liz. *We Wanted You*. Roaring Brook, 2002. Ages five-eight.

Parents tell how they waited and prepared for the child that they wanted so much.

Schreck, Karen H. *Lucy's Family Tree*. Tilbury House, 2001. Ages nine-twelve.

Lucy, an adopted child from Mexico, is convinced that her family background is too complicated for her to make the family tree she is supposed to create for a homework assignment. A multicultural selection.

Stoeke, Janet Morgan. *Waiting for May*. Dutton, 2005. Ages five-eight.

A young boy looks forward to the day when a new sister, who will be adopted from China, joins his family. A multicultural selection.

Thomas, Eliza. *The Red Blanket*. Scholastic Press, 2004. Ages five-seven.

This true story relates the author's journey to China to adopt a baby.

Wilson, Jacqueline. *The Story of Tracy Beaker*. Delacorte Press, 2001. Ages five-eight.

Ten-year-old Tracy, who lives in a children's home because her mother was forced to give her up, dreams of getting a good foster family where she can be happy until her mother comes back for her.

Winter, Jeanette. *Mama: A True Story*. Harcourt, 2006. Ages five-eight.

A true account of a baby hippo who was stranded in the 2004 tsunami and was adopted by a giant male tortoise.

Zisk, Mary. *The Best Single Mom in the World: How I Was Adopted.* Whitman, 2001. Ages five-seven.

> A girl tells how her mother decided to become a single parent and traveled overseas to adopt her and describes their happy life as a family. A multicultural selection.

Professional Resources

Hollyer, Belinda, editor. *The Kingfisher Book of Family Poems.* Kingfisher, 2003.

> This collection features two poems about adoption, "They Chose Me," about a child's adoptive family and birth family and, "Brilliant—Like Me," told from an older sibling's perspective as the family adopts a new baby.

Lanchon, Anne. *All About Adoption: How to Deal with Questions About Your Past.* Abrams/Amulet, 2006.

> Among the topics in this advice book are finding birth parents, why parents adopt, fear of abandonment, insensitive comments about race, and concerns about heredity.

Nemiroff, Marc and Jane Annunziata. *All About Adoption: How Families Are Made and How Kids Feel About It.* Magination, 2004.

> An introduction to adoption that presents information on why birth parents make adoption plans and adoptive parents decide to adopt.

Powell, Jillian. *Talking About Adoption.* Raintree, 2000.

> Written in question and answer format, this book addresses adoption in a factual manner.

Watkins, Mary. *Talking with Young Children About Adoption.* Yale University Press, 1995.

> A clinical psychologist and a psychiatrist, both adoptive mothers, discuss how young children make sense of the fact that they are adopted, how it might appear in their play, and what worries they and their parents may have. Accounts by twenty adoptive parents of conversations about adoption with their children, from ages two to ten, graphically convey what the process of sharing about adoption is like.

Web Connections

Dave Thomas Foundation for Adoption
<http://www.davethomasfoundationforadoption.org/html/resource/index.asp>

> Founder of Wendy's Restaurants, Dave Thomas's site promotes the understanding of adoption and provides extensive information on professional organizations and resources for adoption.

Evan B. Donaldson Adoption Institute

> Adoption professionals can glean a wealth of information on research, policy, and practice from this site.

Chapter 8

Divorce

The Days of Summer

Copyright date: 2001
Author: Eve Bunting
Recommended age range: five to eight
Awards: Kerlan Award, Regina Medal, Southern California Council on Literature for Young People Award

Summary

As Nora and her sister, Jo-Jo, return to school in the fall, they receive the news that their grandparents are getting a divorce.

Discovery and Discussion: Setting the Stage for Reading

- **Words for Review:** fluttered, doleful, starling, gloomy, jiggled, fake, landlord, sobbed, generous

- **Library Skills**

  > Information Literacy Standards: 1, 6, 9
  > NCTE/IRA Standards for English Language Arts: 1, 3, 11, 12

Open to the book's title page. Review the book's title, author, illustrator, and publication information emphasizing the copyright date and its location. Ask students to predict what the story will be about from the cover and title.

- **Directionality**
Have students define the term "family." Ask students to discuss the members of their families. What makes their family unique?

- **Concept Mapping**

  > Information Literacy Standards: 4, 5, 9
  > NCTE/IRA Standards for English Language Arts: 11, 12

Construct a concept map to illustrate family relationships. Include the terminology mother, father, sister, brother, aunt, uncle, grandfather, grandmother. Emphasize the terms grandmother and grandfather. Ask students to define a "grandmother/grandfather." Ask students if any of them have grandparents and how they refer to them, e.g., "Grandma," "Papa."

Exploration: During Reading

■ Vocabulary

Stop periodically to point out the challenging and new words listed in pre-reading vocabulary development. Use the context to help students define those terms. Add new words to the classroom word wall.

Reading Between the Lines: Post Reading

■ Reading Comprehension/Making Connections

> Information Literacy Standards: 3, 6, 9
> NCTE/IRA Standards for English Language Arts: 1, 3, 11, 12

Ask students how the title of the story relates to what happened in the story. Ask students if they think this is an appropriate title for the story. Why/Why not? Go back to the picture on page 22 and think about what is happening in the story.

■ Hidden Message

> Information Literacy Standards: 1, 3, 6
> NCTE/IRA Standards for English Language Arts: 1, 3, 4, 5, 6, 11, 12

Using the pre-reading vocabulary words, have students search for the Hidden Message in Figure 8.1 on page 141. (The answer to the hidden message is the title of the book). After students solve the puzzle, have them write in their journals about why the story is important, what they learned about the characters who are experiencing a divorce, and what they learned about themselves.

Beyond the Text: Lesson Extensions

■ Math Connection

At one point in the story, Jo-Jo remarks that Grandma is teaching her to play dominoes. Teach students to play dominoes. Make sets of dominoes on paper. Rules on how to play can be found at the following Web site:
<www.ehow.com/how_9241_play-dominoes.html>.

■ Grandparents' Day

Plan a grandparents' day at your school. Create and send invitations asking your grandparents to attend. If they live too far away or do not have grandparents, have them invite a relative who is a senior citizen or a neighbor who is a senior citizen. Serve cookies and punch. Have students interview a grandparent, relative, or neighbor regarding past traditions and present their findings to the class.

Hidden Message

Directions: Find the story words in the word search and circle them. The words may run in any direction. After you circle the story words, use the letters that remain to spell out the hidden message. Write the hidden message in the blanks provided.

```
S   D   L   T   H   G   E   D   D
T   E   A   U   A   E   Y   E   S
A   L   R   Y   F   N   R   S   O
R   G   E   O   S   E   F   M   B
L   G   M   S   T   R   L   O   B
I   I   M   T   H   O   U   O   E
N   J   U   M   E   U   M   L   D
G   L   S   E   R   S   O   G   F
F   L   A   N   D   L   O   R   D
```

Word Bank:

DOLEFUL	GLOOM	SOBBED
FLUTTERED	JIGGLED	STARLING
GENEROUS	LANDLORD	

Hidden Message:

Print the hidden message in the blanks below.

___ ___ ___   ___ ___ ___ ___   ___ ___ ___   ___ ___ ___ ___ ___ ___

Two Homes

Copyright date: 2001
Author: Claire Masurel
Recommended age range: four to eight

Discovery and Discussion: Setting the Stage for Reading

Summary

Young Alex describes what it is like to have two of everything including two homes in which to live because his mother and father live apart.

- **Words for Review:** home, one, two, room, love, coat, chair, door

- **Home Drawing Story/Letter-Sound Recognition**

> *Information Literacy Standards: 1, 2, 6, 9*
> *NCTE/IRA Standards for English Language Arts: 3, 11, 12*

Before reading the book, introduce the letter "H" by using the lesson below. Draw the figures on the board or a transparency. Read the words in bold type and draw the figure/letter indicated in parenthesis.

Begin by saying, **"I'm building something. I'd like to tell you and show you what I am building. Can you guess what it is? The thing I am drawing has many windows. I'm going to draw a window here."** (Draw a rectangle.) **"This thing also has water pipes. I need to dig a v-shaped ditch."** (Draw a Capital V to the right of the rectangle.) **"That runs from here to there."** (Make the capital V into a capital M.) **"The thing I am building also has stairs. I'm building three stairs here."** (To the right of the letter M, draw three parallel lines, underneath each other and to the right of the letter M.) **"...and a railing on the side."** (Make the three parallel lines into the capital letter E.) **"Finally, I'm building not one, but two driveways."** (Draw two vertical lines approximately six inches apart to the left of the rectangle.) **"...with a sidewalk between the driveways. Who can tell me what I'm building?"** (Make the two vertical lines into the capital letter H.)

Have students spell the word aloud in unison working on the letter names (h-o-m-e). Have students identify other words in the classroom room that begin with the letter "h." Introduce students to the sound the letter "h" makes. Ask students to identify other words that begin with /h/. (Discussion: Ask students to name rooms in a home and describe the purpose of each room. Ask students to identify items that can be found in certain rooms in a home. For example, what items can be found in a kitchen? What activities take place in the kitchen?

Exploration: During Reading

- **Building Schema**

> *Information Literacy Standards: 1, 2, 3, 6*
> *NCTE/IRA Standards for English Language Arts: 1, 3, 11, 12*

Ask students how the pictures help them to understand what is happening in the story.

■ Picture Clues

While reading the story, pause on pages 12, 13, 18, 19, 20, and 21 and ask students to identify items in the illustrations. Using the Venn diagram in Figure 8.2 on page 144, ask students to compare the items they have in their homes with the items in the illustrations.

Reading Between the Lines: Post Reading

■ Story Elements

Information Literacy Standards: 1, 2, 3, 4, 5, 6
NCTE/IRA Standards for English Language Arts: 1, 3, 4, 11, 12

Make a class list of story elements as you ask students the following:

1. What is the name of the main character in the story?
2. Tell one thing about the character.
3. Have you ever met anyone like this character?
4. How is that person like the main character?
5. How are they different from the main character?
6. Does the story take place over more than one day? How do you know?
7. What happened at the beginning, middle, and end of the story?

■ Word Stairs

List the following words from the story on the board or on a transparency: home, one, two, room, love, coat, chair, and door. Reproduce the Word Stairs in Figure 8.3 on page 145. Have students trace the word, home. To begin the word stairs, have students connect one of the vocabulary words to the word home. Continue the process until a staircase of words has been created from the bottom to the top of the paper.

Beyond the Text: Lesson Extensions

■ Math Connection

Explain the concept of pairs. Have students divide into pairs and count by twos. Students can use the following Web site to learn more about the pair concept and counting by twos: <www.apples4theteacher.com/holidays/100th-day-of-school/counting-by-twos/index.html>. Follow with discussion of items that come in pairs. For example, a pair of shoes or a pair of gloves.

■ Human Go Fish

Information Literacy Standards: 1, 2, 3, 6, 9
NCTE/IRA Standards for English Language Arts: 3, 6, 11, 12

Assign each child a letter, either upper or lower case, to wear for human memory. Write or type the letter in large font on paper or cardstock and use string to make a necklace to hang around each child's neck. Make sure there is the same number of upper case letters as lower case letters. For example, if there are 20 students, there would be ten lower

Picture Clues

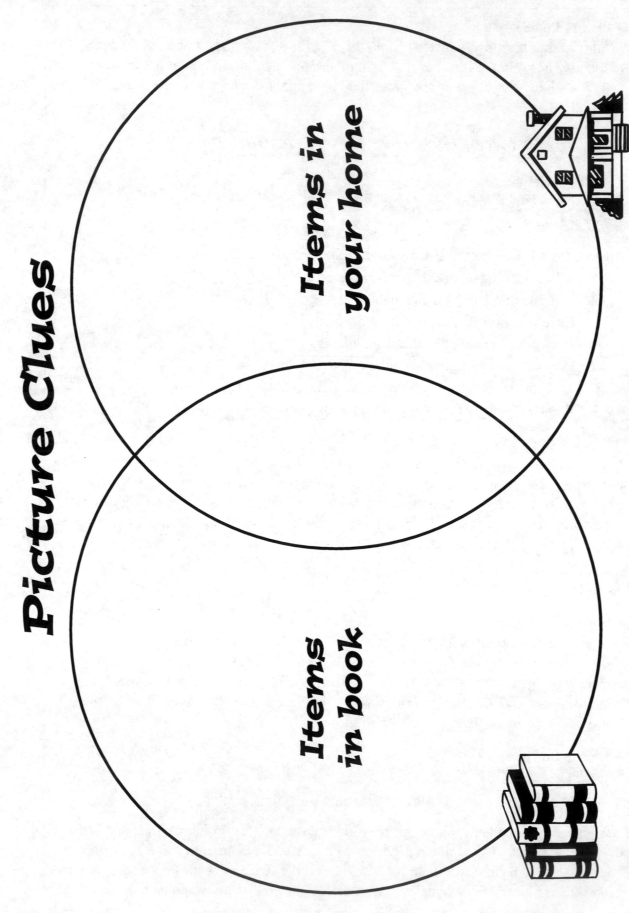

Items in your home

Items in book

© 2006 Inspiration Software®, Inc. Diagram created in Inspiration® Software, Inc. Used with permission.

Picture Clues. Figure 8.2

Word Stairs

Directions: Trace the word "home." Connect one of vocabulary words (one, two, room, love, coat, chair, and door) to the word home. Continue the process until a staircase of words has been created from the bottom to the top of the paper. An example is provided below.

Example:

O
N
HOME

H O M E

Words Stairs. Figure 8.3

case letters and ten upper case letters. Tell students that they are to keep their letters hidden from classmates. While wearing their letters, students stand in a circle and play a version of "Go Fish." Students look for their match by asking their classmates questions without using the name of the letter. An example might be "I am looking for a letter that has the sound /b/. It begins the word bat." If the student they are asking does not have the letter b, they tell them to go fish. They must stand in the middle or some alternative to picking up another card as in the original. This activity reinforces letter identification, upper and lower case letters, and letter sound correspondence.

■ Music Activity

Students can sing the song *Hickory Dickory Dock* and use finger plays to identify the song words. Lyrics are available <www.kididdles.com/mouseum/h046.html>.

■ Designing Houses

Students can work in groups to create graham cracker houses. Houses can be put on display in the library. The recipe, which makes four houses, follows:

Ingredients:

- 12 graham crackers
- 1 batch of royal icing
- 12 tablespoons regular cake frosting
- assorted colored cereals, candies, miniature marshmallows, pretzel sticks

Before class begins, use a knife to score the graham crackers before breaking them into four equal squares. Use the graham crackers to create four walls in each of four structures, using the royal icing squeezed from a pastry bag, to join the sides. When the structure is firm, use two additional graham cracker squares and royal icing to create a roof for each structure. When firm, give one graham cracker house, as well as an assortment of decorations and three tablespoons cake frosting to each student. Have students decorate their house with the decorations using the frosting to glue on the decorations. Royal icing is not regular cake or cookie icing. To make the royal icing combine one and one-third cups confectioner's sugar, one tablespoon meringue powder (available at specialty cake decorating stores), and one and one-half tablespoons warm water. Keep the frosting in a pastry bag.

I Don't Want to Talk about It: A Story About Divorce for Young Children

Copyright date: 2000
Author: Jeanine Franz Ransom
Recommended age range: five to ten

Discovery and Discussion: Setting the Stage for Reading

- **Words for Review:** checkers, pretended, inspect, prickly, mane, disagreement

- **Before We Read**

> Information Literacy Standards: 1, 2, 6, 9
> NCTE/IRA Standards for English Language Arts: 3, 6, 11, 12

Summary

An unnamed young girl reacts to the news about her parents' divorce through metaphorical language to explain her feelings and emotions. Her parents are patient, supportive, and loving throughout the story and work hard to help her adjust. Includes an afterword for helping students through this change.

Read the title of the book aloud to students. Have a student identify the animal on the book's cover. Take a "picture walk" through the book and indicate to students that other animals, birds, and reptiles will be discussed in the story and to listen for specific examples and details as the story is read. Ask a student to read the title of the book again. Ask students, "What does the contraction, 'don't' stand for?" Indicate that many contractions are used throughout the story and to listen for contractual words.

Exploration: During Reading

Simile Discussion

Stop reading periodically to discuss the thoughts and feelings of the young girl. Point out the similes used throughout the story such as "run away like a wild horse" and "prickly like a porcupine." Explain to students that similes are a comparison between two things using the words "like" or "as."

Reading Between the Lines: Post Reading

Adopt an Animal

> Information Literacy Standards: 2, 3, 4
> NCTE/IRA Standards for English Language Arts: 4, 5, 6, 11, 12

Review the animals in the story. Pose the question, "If you were to adopt one of these animals, which one would you adopt and why?" Have students write their responses in their journal. As a class project, students can adopt a class pet virtually. The following Web sites provide information on adopting a class pet and class pet exchange: <http://teacherweb.com/IN/PNC/Cassady/h1.stm> and <http://classroom.jc-schools.net/cpe/welcome.html>.

■ Animal Facts

Information Literacy Standards: 1, 2, 3, 6, 8
NCTE/IRA Standards for English Language Arts: 1, 4, 5, 6, 7, 8, 11, 12

Review the animals in the story. Using the Electronic Zoo Web site, <http://netvet.wustl.edu/e-zoo.htm>, have students find three facts about each of the animals. Using chart paper, compose a class list of the animal facts for display in classroom or library. For younger students, this can be completed as a whole group.

■ Similes

Information Literacy Standards: 3, 5
NCTE/IRA Standards for English Language Arts: 4, 6, 11, 12

Point out the similes in the story (like a wild horse, like an elephant). In their journal have students complete the prompt, "Clouds are like…" For older students ask them to compose original simile sentences to share with the class. Provide sentence strips for students' sentences to be displayed throughout the classroom or library.

■ Using Adjectives/Alphabetical Order

Information Literacy Standards: 3, 5
NCTE/IRA Standards for English Language Arts: 4, 6, 11, 12

Explain that adjectives are words that answer the questions: Which one? How many? What kind? Continue to explain that adjectives make the story more colorful and interesting and help them "see" a story in their imagination using their mind's eye. Return to the story and have students pick out adjectives that describe each of the animals and make a class list. Have students put the words in alphabetical order.

■ Caboose

Information Literacy Standards: 1, 3, 9
NCTE/IRA Standards for English Language Arts: 4, 6, 11, 12

The objective of this strategy is to encourage vocabulary enrichment while emphasizing spelling. Divide students into two teams and follow these procedures:

1. Announce the category is describing animals and no words can be repeated.
2. The first student in team one gives the name of an animal, e.g., dog, and spells the word.
3. The first student on team two must give an adjective that describes a dog using the last letter of the word (in this case dog) and spells the word.
4. The next student on team two now gives a word from the animal category and a student in team one must give an adjective using the last letter of the animal category word.
5. Continue to alternate until everyone has a turn.
6. Award points for each word that is spelled correctly.

■ Using Story Words (grades one and up)

Information Literacy Standards: 1, 3, 9
NCTE/IRA Standards for English Language Arts: 4, 6, 11, 12

Have students complete the Story Words found in Figure 8.4 on page 150 by writing each of the story words under its correct heading. After students have categorized the words, have students alphabetize the list of words. When students have completed this task, have students choose one of the two categories, nouns or verbs, and write a story in their journal using all the words in that category.

■ Writing Sentences with Contractions (grades two and up)

Information Literacy Standards: 1, 2, 3, 6
NCTE/IRA Standards for English Language Arts: 4, 5, 6, 11, 12

Because numerous contractions are used throughout the story, this strategy enables students to understand the meaning of contractions. Students see that two words and their contraction can be used interchangeably in the same sentence. Using Figure 8.5 on page 151, Sentences with Contractions, have students circle the correct substitution for the underlined word or words.

Beyond the Text: Lesson Extensions

■ Online Zoo Visit

Information Literacy Standards: 1, 2, 3, 6, 8
NCTE/IRA Standards for English Language Arts: 4, 5, 6, 7, 8, 11, 12

Have students visit the virtual zoo site, <http://library.thinkquest.org/11922/> and make a list of their five favorite exhibits and explain in paragraph form in their journal why these are their favorite exhibits.

■ Synonyms and Antonyms (grades one and up)

Information Literacy Standards: 1, 3
NCTE/IRA Standards for English Language Arts: 4, 6, 11, 12

Discuss synonyms and antonyms with students by giving several examples. Introduce the thesaurus as the "synonym/antonym dictionary." Have students use the thesaurus to complete the skill sheet in Figure 8.6 on page 152, Synonyms and Antonyms. The skill sheet can be done individually, with partners, or as a whole class depending on students' abilities.

Story Words

Directions: Review the story words in the table below. Decide if each word is a noun or verb and write the word in the appropriate column. Next, alphabetize the words in each column.

pocket	live	grave	garden
reached	river	gobble	parents
toss	houses	window	stood
home	toss	night	door
book	read	hear	fingers
telephone	father	believe	stop
believe	hair	run	mother
gooble	week	hoped	horse

Nouns	Verbs
Alphabetize the words below.	Alphabetize the words below.

Story Words. Figure 8.4

Sentences with Contractions

Directions: Circle the correct substitution for the underlined word or words and rewrite the sentence using the correct contraction. The first one is done for you.

Sentence	Circle the correct answer.		Rewrite the sentence using the contraction
Example *I am 10 years old.*	*I'll*	*(I'm)*	*I'm 10 years old.*
Jason does not want to adopt the turtle.	doesn't	don't	
I will be living in the country.	I'll	I'd	
They will live in a farmhouse.	They're	They'll	
Check your watch to find out how much time we will have to do our homework.	we'll	we've	
He is happy that you came to the zoo with me.	He's	He've	
Tell me which book you have read.	You've	You'd	
I can not go to school because I am sick.	can't	can'd	
Justin has not been to the National Zoo.	has've	hasn't	
That glass of juice is not yours.	isn't	its	
If dad says I can have a pet, I will get a cat.	I'll	I've	

Sentences with Contractions. Figure 8.5

Synonyms and Antonyms

Directions: Write a synonym for the story word in column 2. Write an antonym for the story word in column 3. An example is given.

Story Word	Synonym	Antonym
Example: *sad*	*unhappy*	*glad*
stop		
big		
fast		
quiet		
always		
wonderful		
loud		
nightly		
gently		

Synonyms and Antonyms. Figure 8.6

Additional Book Selections, Professional Resources, and Web Connections on Divorce

Bauer, Joan. *Stand Tall.* Putnam, 2002. Ages nine-twelve.
Tree, a six-foot-three-inch twelve-year-old, copes with his parents' recent divorce and his failure as an athlete by helping his grandfather, a Vietnam vet and recent amputee, and Sophie, a new girl at school. Newbery Author.

Bernhard, Durga. *To and Fro, Fast and Slow.* Walker, 2001. Ages five-seven.
A girl who is shuttled between the homes of her divorced parents observes such opposites as "over, under," "rainy, sunny," and "full, empty."

Blume, Judy. *It's Not the End of the World.* Yearling, 1986. Ages nine-twelve.
When her parents divorce, a sixth grader struggles to understand that sometimes people are unable to live together.

Brown, Laurene Krasny and Marc Brown. *Dinosaurs Divorce: A Guide for Changing Families.* Little, Brown, 1986. Ages five-nine.
Text and illustrations of dinosaur characters introduce aspects of divorce such as its causes and effects, living with a single parent, spending holidays in two separate households, and adjusting to a stepparent.

Bunting, Eve. *Some Frog.* Voyager, 2003. Ages six-nine.
Billy is disappointed when his father does not show up to help him catch a frog for the frog-jumping competition at school, but the one he and his mother catch wins the championship and Billy begins to accept his father's absence.

Caseley, Judith. *Priscilla Twice.* Greenwillow, 1995. Ages five-eight.
When Priscilla's parents divorce, she learns that there are different kinds of families.

Christopher, Matt. *The Comeback Challenge.* Little, Brown, 1996. Ages nine-twelve.
Mark, who is the center for his middle school's soccer team, must cope with his parents' divorce and a teammate who holds a grudge against him. A multicultural selection.

Cleary, Beverly. *Dear Mr. Henshaw.* HarperTrophy, 2000, Ages nine-twelve.
In his letters to his favorite author, ten-year-old Leigh reveals his problems in coping with his parents' divorce, being the new boy in school, and generally finding his own place in the world. Newbery Award.

Coy, John. *Two Old Potatoes and Me.* Knopf, 2003. Ages five-eight.
A divorced father and his daughter plant two old potatoes and watch them grow.

Danziger, Paula. *Amber Brown Is Feeling Blue.* Scholastic, 1999. Ages seven-ten.
Nine-year-old Amber Brown faces further complications because of her parents' divorce when her father plans to move back from Paris and she must decide which parent she will be with on Thanksgiving.

Ford, Jan Blackstone, et al. *My Parents Are Divorced, Too: A Book for Kids by Kids.* Ages seven-twelve.
Three stepsiblings in a blended family discuss their experiences and those of friends with divorce and remarriage.

Gallagher, Mary Collins. *Ginny Morris and Dad's New Girlfriend.* Magination Press, 2006. Ages seven-ten.

> Just as Ginny begins to think that her divorced parents might like one another again, she learns that her father has a girlfriend, and the mixture of feelings this stirs up causes trouble at home and school.

Gallagher, Mary Collins. *Ginny Morris and Mom's House, Dad's House.* Magination Press, 2005. Ages seven-ten.

> Ginny Morris is in the fourth grade and her parents have been divorced for two years. She goes back and forth between her mother's apartment and her father's house, switching each Sunday.

Girard, Linda W. *At Daddy's on Saturdays.* Whitman, 1991. Ages five-eight.

> Although her parents' divorce causes her to feel anger, concern, and sadness, Katie discovers that she can keep a loving relationship with her father even though he lives apart from her.

Krementz, Jill. *How It Feels When Parents Divorce.* Fireside, 1996.

> Boys and girls share their feelings about their parents' divorce.

Lansky, Vicki. *It's Not Your Fault, Koko Bear.* Book Peddlers, 1998. Ages five-eight.

> KoKo Bear learns what divorce means, how to deal with changes, how to recognize and talk about her feelings, and that the divorce is not her fault. Each page includes tips for parents.

Levins, Sandra. *Was It the Chocolate Pudding? A Story for Little Kids About Divorce.* Magination Press, 2006. Ages five-eight.

> When a young boy's parents divorce, he thinks it is because of the chocolate pudding he and his brother smeared all over the wall. He learns this is not the reason.

Lowry, Danielle. *What Can I Do? A Book for Children of Divorce.* Magination Press, 2001. Ages five-eight.

> This story can help children understand and work through their feelings about the reality of divorce.

Paterson, Katherine. *The Same Stuff as Stars.* HarperTrophy, 2004. Ages nine-twelve.

> When Angel's self-absorbed mother leaves her and her younger brother with their poor great-grandmother, the eleven-year-old girl worries not only about her mother and brother, her imprisoned father, the frail old woman, but also about a mysterious man who begins sharing with her the wonder of the stars. Newbery Award winning author.

Pickhardt, Carl E. *The Case of the Scary Divorce.* Magination Press, 1998. Ages nine-twelve.

> A ten-year-old boy meets the mysterious "Professor Jackson Skye: Helping Investigator" who enlists his aid in solving eight cases, each dealing with a problem he himself is experiencing during his parents' divorce.

Rogers, Fred. *Let's Talk About It: Divorce.* Putnam, 1998. Ages five-eight.

> This well known author provides helpful advice to children who are facing the changes divorce brings to a family.

Simon, Norma. *All Families Are Special.* Whitman, 2003. Ages five-eight.

> When a teacher asks her students to tell about their families, each child speaks of a different configuration. A multicultural selection.

Spelman, Cornelia M. *Mama and Daddy Bear's Divorce.* Whitman, 2001. Ages five-seven.

> Dinah Bear feels sad and scared when her parents say they are going to divorce.

Stern, Zoe and Evan. *Divorce Is Not the End of the World: Zoe's And Evan's Coping Guide for Kids.* Tricycle Press, 1997. Ages nine-twelve.

> A brother and sister whose parents are divorced discuss topics relating to this situation, respond to letters from children, and offer tips based on their experience. Includes insights from their mother.

Thomas, Pat. *My Family's Changing.* Barron, 1999. Ages five-eight.

> As the title indicates, this story introduces the idea and process of a divorce, as well as discusses how it often affects the members of the family.

Wilson, Jacqueline. *The Suitcase Kid.* Yearling, 1998. Ages eight-twelve.

> Ten-year-old Andrea tries to deal with her parents' divorce and the presence of stepparents, stepsisters, and stepbrothers.

Winchester, Kent and Roberta Beyer. *What in the World Do You Do When Your Parents Divorce? A Survival Guide for Kids.* Free Spirit, 2001. Ages seven-twelve.

> A simple and honest approach to explain divorce, new living arrangements, and other basics to help children understand what is happening in their lives. The story helps students realize that divorce isn't their fault, strong emotions are okay, and families can survive difficult changes.

Professional Resources

Beyer, Roberta and Kent Winchester. *Speaking of Divorce: How to Talk with Your Kids and Help Them Cope.* Free Spirit, 2001.

> The authors offers many proven communication techniques to explain this sensitive topic to children.

Neuman, M. Gary. *Helping Your Kids Cope with Divorce the Sandcastles Way.* Random House, 1999.

> More than a hundred pieces of artwork from children of divorced parents that express their emotions and how they perceive the experience. Special activities to help communicate with children are also included.

Schneider, Meg F. *Difficult Questions Kids Ask and Are Afraid to Ask About Divorce.* Fireside, 1996.

> The author explores the apparent and hidden fears that haunt children as they weather the confusion of a divorce.

Web Connections

Children and Divorce
> Extensive resources on divorce can be found on this site that also offers state-specific articles, an online community, and a nationwide directory of divorce information.

Family Life
<http://hec.osu.edu/famlife/family/divorce3.htm>
> This site contains numerous research-based articles on helping children cope with divorce and single-family homes.

HelpGuide: Children and Separation / Divorce
<www.helpguide.org/mental/children_divorce.htm>
> Developed and reviewed by professionals in the field, this site offers a plethora of information on divorce.

Bibliography

Advanced Learning Technologies in Education Consortia. *Rubistar.* Retrieved December 22, 2005 from <http://rubistar.4teachers.org/index.php>.

Alvermann, Donna E., et al. *Using Discussion to Promote Reading Comprehension.* Newark, DE: International Reading Association, 1987.

American Association of School Librarians and Association for Educational Communications and Technology. *Information Power: Building Partnerships for Learning.* Chicago: American Library Association, 1988.

Anderson, Eric M. *Eric's Origami Page.* Retrieved December 18, 2005 from <www.paperfolding.com/diagrams/>.

Ashton-Warner, Sylvia. *Teacher.* New York: Simon & Schuster, 1965.

Bear, Donald R., et al. *Words Their Way: Word Study for Phonics, Vocabulary, and Spelling Instruction.* Upper Saddle River, NJ: Merrill/Prentice Hall, 1996.

Best of Scrapbook Tips. Retrieved August 20, 2005 from <www.scrapbook.lifetips.com/>.

Cibrowski, Jean. *Textbooks and the Students Who Can't Read Them.* Cambridge, MA: Brookline Books, 1993.

Cunningham, Patricia M. *Phonics They Use.* 2nd ed. New York: HarperCollins, 1995.

Fowler, Gerald L. "Developing Comprehension Skills in Primary Students through the Use of Story Frames." *The Reading Teacher.* November, 1982:176-179.

Gillet, Jean W. and Charles Temple. *Understanding Reading Problems*: *Assessment and Instruction.* Boston: Little, Brown, 1982.

How to Get the Paper Crane. The 1000 Cranes Project. Retrieved November 6, 2005 from <www.csi.ad.jp/suzuhari-es/1000cranes/paperc/>.

International Reading Association and National Council of Teachers of English. *Standards for the English Language Arts.* Washington, DC: International Reading Association, 1996.

Jones, Raymond. *Reading Quest Strategies.* Retrieved May 2, 2005 from <http://curry.edschool.virginia.edu/go/readquest/strat/>.

Lebow, David. "Constructivist Values for Instructional System Design: Five Principles toward a New Mindset." *Educational Technology Research and Development.* Spring, 1992:4-16.

Lee, Dorris. M. and R. V. Allen. *Learning to Read Through Experience.* 2nd ed. New York: Meredith, 1963.

Lyman, Frank. "The Responsive Classroom Discussion: The Inclusion of All Students." In *Mainstreaming Digest.* Ed. A. S. Anderson. College Park, MD: University of Maryland, 1981.

McCormick, Thomas W. *Theories of Reading in Dialogue: An Interdisciplinary Study.* New York: University Press of America, 1988.

McTighe, Jay and Frank T. Lyman. "Cueing Thinking in the Classroom: The Promise of Theory-Embedded Tools." *Educational Leadership.* April, 1988:18-24.

Metzgar, Margaret M. *Developmental Considerations Concerning Children's Grief,* Retrieved May 5, 2005 from <www.kidsource.com/sids/childrensgrief.html>.

Ogle, Donna S. "K-W-L: A Teaching Model That Develops Active Reading of Expository Text." *The Reading Teacher.* February, 1986: 564-570.

Reutzel, D. Ray and Robert B. Cooter. *The Essentials of Teaching Children to Read: What Every Teacher Needs to Know.* Upper Saddle River, NJ: Merrill/Prentice Hall, 2005.

Santrock, John W. *Child Development.* 9th ed. Boston: McGraw-Hill, 2001.

Sowers, S. *The Story and the All-About Book.* In J. Hansen, T. Newkirk, and D. Graves, (Eds.), Breaking Ground: Teachers Relate Reading and Writing in the Elementary School (pp. 73-82). Portsmouth, NH: Heinemann, 1985.

Stauffer, Russell G. *Directing the Reading-Thinking Process.* New York: Harper & Row, 1970.

Tompkins, Gail E. *50 Literacy Strategies: Step By Step.* Upper Saddle River, NJ: Merrill/Prentice Hall, 1998.

Tompkins, Gail E. *Literacy for the 21st Century.* 3rd ed. Upper Saddle River, NJ: Merrill/Prentice Hall, 2003.

Tompkins, Gail E. *Teaching Writing: Balancing Process and Product.* 4th ed. Upper Saddle River, NJ: Merrill/Prentice Hall, 2004.

Wolfelt, Alan D. *Healing Your Grieving Heart: 100 Practical Ideas for Kids.* Fort Collins, CO: Companion Press, 2001.

Title Index

Author Index